The Essex Triangle

The Essex Triangle

*Four decades of violence and mayhem
in a sleepy pocket of rural England*

DAVID THURLOW

ROBERT HALE · LONDON

Robert Hale Limited
Clerkenwell House
Clerkenwell Green
London EC1R 0HT

ISBN 0 7090 4137 3

Photoset in North Wales by
Derek Doyle & Associates, Mold, Clwyd.
Printed in Great Britain by
St Edmundsbury Press, Bury St Edmunds, Suffolk.
and bound by Woolnough.

Contents

Acknowledgements

I covered many of these murders as a reporter. For assistance on some of the others I thank Michael Fielder and Peter Steele for allowing me to use their book *The Barn Murder* as an aid, Derek Drew and Michael Horsnell for help and my colleagues in *The Times* library for assistance.

My thanks to *The Times* for permission to reproduce the letters on pp. 69–72 and the obituary of Maynard Greville (pp. 165–6); to Lord Bonham-Carter for allowing me to reproduce his mother's letters (pp.71–2); and the *Daily Mirror* for permission to reproduce its leader (pp. 72–3).

In some cases where indicated, the names have been changed to save distress after all these years.

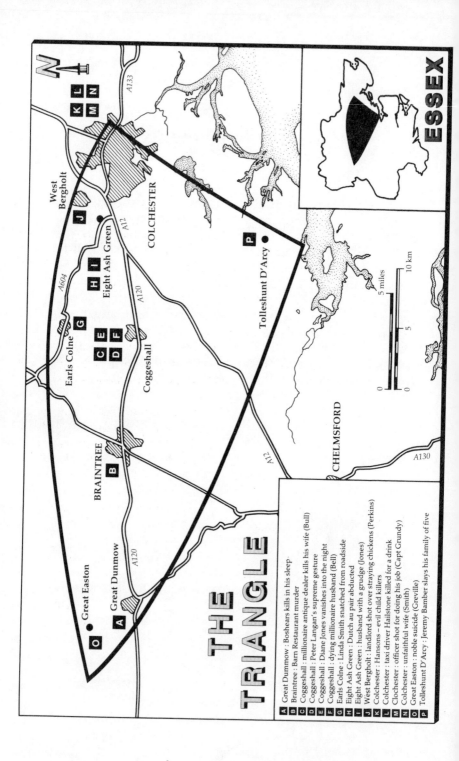

THE TRIANGLE

ESSEX

N

West Bergholt

COLCHESTER

Great Easton

Great Dunmow

BRAINTREE

Earls Colne

Eight Ash Green

Coggeshall

Tolleshunt D'Arcy

CHELMSFORD

A133

A12

A604

A120

A130

5 miles

10 km

A Great Dunmow : Boshears kills in his sleep

B Braintree : Barn Restaurant murder

C Coggeshall : millionaire antique dealer kills his wife (Bull)

D Coggeshall : Peter Langan's supreme gesture

E Coggeshall : Diane Jones vanishes into the night

F Coggeshall : dying millionaire husband (Bell)

G Earls Colne : Linda Smith snatched from roadside

H Eight Ash Green : Dutch au pair abducted

I Eight Ash Green : husband with a grudge (Jones)

J West Bergholt : landlord shot over straying chickens (Perkins)

K Colchester : Hansons – evil child killers

L Colchester : taxi driver Hailstone killed for a drink

M Clochester : officer shot for doing his job (Capt Grundy)

N Colchester : unfaithful wife (Smith)

O Great Easton : noble suicide (Greville)

P Tolleshunt D'Arcy : Jeremy Bamber slays his family of five

Introduction

There are some people, places and events so famous that there is no need to add any means of identification. Sinatra, Crosby, the Beatles, Belsen, Dunkirk, Hiroshima, Stalin, Churchill, Pearl Harbor, Jagger, Mickey Mouse, Pink Panther, D-Day, ET, Pele, Maradona, Real Madrid, Garland, Fitzgerald, Rogers & Hammerstein, Himmler, Hitler, Lee Harvey Oswald, Lloyd-Webber, Kennedy, Dallas. Some are internationally famous, others just nationally. Occasionally in Britain some high court judge earns himself publicity by asking 'Who are the Beatles?' and those in court laugh to curry favour and in embarrassment. Most only have to hear the name to know exactly who the place or person is.

Crime is not so universal. In the first half of this century when the pace of life was not so fast, a major murder did cross the Channel and sometimes the Atlantic and names like Christie, Al Capone, Bluebeard, Lindberg, Dreyfus became known, certainly to the English-speaking world.

Now terrorist criminals are the only ones who are internationally known and even then it is often by different names. No one is that interested. But in Britain there are names that are so infamous that even in the age of television they hit a note in the memory.

Some say it is odd that they should do so but everyone is fascinated by crime. It may well be the victims, the witness, the family involved that attracts them to the event and make them read what it is about. But it is well known that Newgate means prison, particularly for debtors; that Dartmoor is the most evil of prisons even though it is now low category; that the Moors Murders were evil beyond belief; 10 Rillington Place was where Christie performed his mass killings and used a victim's hip bone to hold up the fence; Tyburn is famous for hanging, Jeffries for mass hanging; the Old Bailey for dramatic trials and Ruth Ellis as the last woman to hang for a crime of passion for good (or bad) measure.

The Essex Triangle has not yet achieved such notoriety although it may soon do so if the rate of crime continues at its present pace. It is extraordinary that there is no other area of Britain where such a catalogue of crime bizarre and outrageous has taken place. Major cities have large numbers of crimes of violence, missing people, domestic killings – some appalling, like the wife who took revenge on her husband's young lover by recruiting her family and gluing the girl's mouth before stabbing her and throwing her into the Thames – but they do not match the consistency of the Triangle in strangeness.

It is a small parcel of land in rural Essex, enclosed mainly by Roman roads, where people lead normal lives in towns and villages. There are pubs and restaurants, shops and stores but nothing big, nothing to suggest a fast pace of life, nothing other than the tranquillity one expects from rolling farmland and copses and silent evenings where the inhabitants tend to stay indoors and let the traffic and the world roar by.

But what goes on behind those doors that sends a man out to take a teenage girl from the side of the road and drive her through quiet country lanes to beat her to death with a blunt heavy instrument on a frosty January night? She was Dutch and in a foreign country but she must have known him otherwise there was no point in killing her to keep her quiet. A casual passing motorist would have thrown her out and driven on.

It is the same with the snatching of a little eleven-year-old girl from the roadside in the Triangle. Only a local man would have known the back route through the lanes to dump her when she protested at what he was trying to do. It must have been someone she knew because there was no point in killing her otherwise. He could have pushed her out as he drove or pulled up and pushed her out. Murder, without even having the sex one must presume he wanted, was a capital crime then.

And what of the American serviceman who in his sleep strangled a girl he had taken home and claimed that he had dreamt it? Or the millionaire antique-dealer whose customers included VIPs who killed his wife in case he might lose his share of the money, or the adopted son who slaughtered five for money?

Then there were the incompetent robbers, one of whom was a homicidal maniac, who went to a popular restaurant on Guy Fawkes night to steal and ended up in a case of identification that made legal history. Not too far away the biggest fence in Britain was stuffed into his car, a corpse with bullets in his head to swell balloon-shape in the heat; killed for what?

These are just some of the major crimes committed in the Triangle. Similar may be found elsewhere in the country but not together. On top of these are the cases of the international restaurateur who threatened to pour petrol round his wife after they had made love, the army couple who enjoyed weird sex and used a child for their game that ended in murder, the amazing domestic killings that were not in a fit of temper but in deep hatred, the callous killers of an old lady and a taxidriver, and the doctor's wife who liked drink and men when in it, who vanished in her drive and did not turn up again for three months when she was found murdered in a field miles away.

It is a collection of crime that is unique to one area. One or two more of similar ilk and the tiny envelope of rural England will become as notorious as the killing fields of Germany and Poland.

So what is it that makes this area as it is? What clues can we find from its make-up? This is the character, the background to the sad but fascinating and ghastly stories to follow:

The Triangle is bounded on two sides by great Roman roads, stretching out like webs from Colchester, the ancient capital of England. One side stretches from Colchester along the line of Icknield Street for just a short distance to Lexden before bearing north-west up the Via Devana (now the A604) towards Cambridge, going a little south so the line slightly curves, and on to Great Dunmow, a distance of around twenty-three miles.

The next side of about twenty-five miles runs south

across country land with an agricultural roll, south to the old Stane Street (now the A130 which runs from Dunmow through Braintree and on to Colchester) in a line which takes it below Witham to Tolleshunt D'Arcy, named after the fifteenth-century family that lived there and the largest but not the oldest of the Tolleshunts. That is Tolleshunt Major, the only one in the Domesday Book.

The final and shortest side, a little over ten miles, runs back to Colchester.

Lying half-way along the longest side of the Triangle is Coggeshall, a town of 4,000 people, once a major town when the Flemish wool and silk weavers came up the River Blackwater in the fifteenth and sixteenth centuries, once a breeding ground of witches where the last was burnt in 1755 and now a town renowned for antique shops, seed-making and murder most foul. It is in the hub of the Triangle, the place where murders have taken place and one on which one can focus and ask why, in this so rural part of England, so many and bizarre affairs of violence occur.

The town goes back to Roman days and stands on Stane Street, the modern version of which runs through the village, dividing it in two, crossing the River Blackwater in the centre of town. It is a lovely place, everything that a foreigner imagines an English country town to be, with sixteenth-, seventeenth- and eighteenth-century half-timbered houses lovingly washed in white or green or pink and even blue, some joined together in a row, others on their own. The most attractive and most famous is Paycocke House, built at the end of the 1440s and left to his son Thomas by wool merchant and clothier John Paycocke. It is now owned by the National Trust and thousands of visitors from all over the world wander along the main street to visit and admire it.

It fits the atmosphere perfectly in a town where antique shops are so plentiful that the sign on the main road pointing to the town advertises the fact. The air of prosperity which languished in the eighteenth century when the wool and silk merchants moved away still exists with farmers and seed merchants and wives, driving BMWs and Mercedes, shopping and dining in the square and area around it.

But underneath this genuine polish hangs an air, a pattern of eccentricity, odd behaviour, some might justifiably say evil too, that goes back three hundred years and more.

Some call it the Curse of Coggeshall, tying it in with the witches hunted out by Matthew Hopkins, a lawyer from Manningtree which is outside the Triangle, who went round the county with an assistant and a young woman in the eighteenth century. They searched for witch marks before pointing the accusing finger which sent the witch in question to the stake for incineration.

Or perhaps it is perversity. There was an uprising against a poll tax which was imposed in 1380 and caused trouble all over the south of England. It was hated much as it is today but then the agricultural workers took strong action against the decision to impose a charge of three groats per person for everyone over fifteen. In Coggeshall dozens of workers burst into the sheriff's house and burnt his papers.

More likely it is the strange things that people did, odd acts and strange jests and japes known throughout the county as Coggeshall Jobs. They were recorded in 1670 in the rhyme:

> Braintree for the pure and Bocking for the poor,
> Coggeshall for the jeering tom and Kelvedon for the whore.

All four places are in the Triangle.

The reputation has stuck with good cause. When the clock struck only eleven one eighteenth-century noon a villager rode to nearby Lexden where they had heard the clock strike thirteen and brought back the missing stroke – the hand of the clock.

When the town raised an army of volunteers for the Napoleonic Wars no one wanted to be just a plain soldier. They all wanted to be officers so that is what they became.

Once someone in the street told the band rehearsing in a room of a house that they sounded wonderful so they all trooped out in the streets to listen too. Then there was the man who lit fires under his trees to ripen the fruit more quickly, the bride who was told she was beautiful when asleep and closed her eyes when looking in the mirror, the housewives who turned out in force with their brooms when the river flooded to try to sweep the waters back and others who put up blankets to stop the wind blowing the plague into town. When the church was built the architect forgot to put in windows so the townspeople caught the light in their hampers and took them in to the church and opened them to give light.

They also took down one of the two windmills because they did not think there was enough wind for two and a group lifted a bull over the gate to his field, forgetting it could walk. A strange past which could give a reason for some turning evil rather than just odd.

Great Dunmow is another town which has a history with a difference. It is renowned for its Flitch, the annual contest dating back to Henry III for a flitch of prime bacon awarded to the couple who can claim and prove that they have not quarrelled in their marriage.

It is also famous for the great pump row which happened in 1786 when the authorities decided to remove the water pump outside the Saracen's Head Hotel (which is still very much in business) because they considered it a traffic hazard! Three times they removed the pump and filled in the well and three times the townspeople put it back. Eventually enough was enough and the Riot Act was read and some of the locals landed in the dock down the road at Chelmsford at the assizes where they were all sentenced to six months.

Then there is Earls Colne where the Benedictines founded a priory nine hundred years ago, where the earls of Oxford and the wealthy de Veres lived and died and where their tombs were in a local farmhouse for decades until they were removed over the border into Suffolk.

There is also a pump, erected by the villagers in the nineteenth century as a thanksgiving memorial after an epidemic of cholera swept through Essex but somehow missed their tight community.

And Braintree, side by side with Bocking (where Samuel Courtauld from Huguenot stock created artificial silk) comes into this macabre story too. Two Roman roads meet there and Roman bricks built the church. Its great international claim to fame is its famous son Thomas Crittal, renowned for his windows.

Just over the border into Suffolk is Polstead where one of the most infamous murders in British history took place, the slaying of Maria Marten in the Red Barn, literally at the hands of her lover William Corder. It was also the dumping ground for a little girl of eleven, snatched as she went to the shops in the Triangle.

The sum of the history of these places, however, yields nothing on which one can put a finger to explain why it should be a thriving centre of murder. There are hints, clues, the geographical connecting link, but no human reason really why it should be. Or is there?

Consider for yourselves.

1

Boshears

The Nightmare That Was True

American Air Force Staff Sergeant Willis Eugene Boshears was a stocky man of twenty-nine who had a New Year's Day dream that landed him in an assize court dock facing a capital murder charge. And in 1961 that meant hanging if he was found guilty.

It was never meant to happen that way when Boshears, father of three children, set off to celebrate New Year's Eve in Braintree. His Scots wife Jean was north of the border celebrating Hogmanay and he was left on his own with Christmas duties at his base, the sprawling RAF Wethersfield, home of several USAF NATO fighter squadrons.

The Boshears lived in a flat in a large house in Great Dunmow, home of the famous Flitch ceremony for the happiest couple of the year. He spent his free time while his wife was away in the pubs of Braintree, particularly those which catered for the Americans and the girls who liked to be with the easy-going, high-spending American servicemen, often lonely boys far away from home and with plenty of money to spend.

Boshears had been busy socializing while his wife was away in the week after Christmas. He had met an attractive local girl called Jean Constable, aged twenty, and taken her back to the flat. Boshears swore that nothing had ever happened, that someone else had been present, that they had just had a drink.

Jean was described by those who knew her as a party girl, an English rose who loved the good life and Americans. On New Year's Eve she had been invited to go with some Americans to a party in London and when she left her home that is where her parents thought she was going.

But instead she stayed in her home town and during her partying from pub to pub met a young man called David. They stayed together until they came across Boshears in a pub off the market square half an hour before the New Year of 1961. They saw in the New Year in a great wave of nostalgic, alcoholic *Auld Lang Syne* and then Boshears suggested they went back to his flat.

They caught a taxi in the square and were driven the ten miles. At that time Boshears was relatively sober, Jean a bit merry and David had had the most to drink; but no one was in any way drunk. Back at the flat Boshears put his gramophone on and poured out the drinks. The music was loud and they danced and laughed and celebrated too loudly because another American, a sergeant who lived in the flat above them, came down to ask Boshears to turn down his music, which he did.

David was dancing with Jean when Boshears cut in and they danced together. But when Boshears went out of the room the girl went over to the Englishman and made it quite clear what she wanted. They had sex on the mattress which was on the floor and were still there when Boshears came back. He made no fuss but asked if they wanted to see round the house and when the others agreed he showed them the bedroom where once again Jean and David had sex.

A little while later Boshears came in and suggested they all went into the lounge where he had laid the mattress in front of the fire and had some vodka to drink. The American and the girl lay on the mattress apart and it was then that David said he was going home. Boshears told him where to get a taxi and when David asked Jean if she wanted to go home she said no, that she was cosy and comfy and too tired.

Later on in the night, the wife of the American sergeant upstairs heard the sound of a girl crying or sobbing, saying something like 'you don't love me' and the sobs were muffled as if she was holding a handkerchief to her mouth.

into Suffolk, bleeding from the wound, and finally collapsed and died in hospital. If he had had medical treatment earlier he would have lived because he simply bled to death. Instead he died and luckily a British doctor had made a superficial examination before the Americans arrived to demand the body, which they were given. That was the last the British saw of it because it was flown back to America. The wife was acquitted after a masterly defence by the then Michael Havers QC, on the verge of a political life which led him to be Lord Chancellor.

This was thus their attitude and no one was surprised when Major Carl Prestin asked that Boshears be handed over to US custody. 'We will produce him at any place and at any time you specify,' he said. But the local superintendent was not having that. He said, 'I object to that and ask for a remand in civil custody.'

The bench under the chairmanship of Lady Plummer agreed that the British should have him. Boshears was asked if he wanted legal aid and he said that he already had that from the air force.

Then the superintendent told how Jean's partly clothed body was found and inquiries at the American base led them to Boshears who now sat quietly dressed in fur-lined parka, green combat suit and boots.

He was remanded in custody for eight days and no one was any the wiser about what had happened because Inspector Jeavons said he did not propose to reveal it at that stage.

But when the sergeant appeared at Essex assizes at Chelmsford in early February (for in those days the time between arrest and trial was very short indeed – now he would have had to wait around a year) the story was finally told.

It was amazing, ridiculous, unique, staggering, quite extraordinary, a defence that had never been used before. When those in the court heard it there was a gasp of astonishment.

Boshears dreamt that he strangled Jean in his sleep and when he woke up he found that he had actually done so; his dream became a nightmare because there he was in an empty flat with his wife and children away and the dead body of a girl whom he knew he had strangled because he had dreamt that he had.

And so he panicked. He sat for two days not knowing what to do and then finally he decided that he must get rid of the body. Not only that, but he must remove any identifying articles from her. He took off most of her clothes and then in macabre fashion by firelight cut off much of her hair and finally took off her rings and jewellery. Then he took her, wrapped in his coat, down the stairs, put her in the boot of his car and drove along the Cambridge road and just dumped her under a wild rose bush at a spot called Ashleigh Meadows at Ridgewell. He drove home and sat and waited for the inevitable.

That was in essence what Mr Stanley Rees QC, prosecuting, told the jury in the assize court where press and public packed to hear what it was all about.

David was the first witness after Boshears had pleaded not guilty and the jury had had the facts outlined to them.

David told how he met Jean whom he had not known before and then later Boshears before going back to the flat in Dunmow where they drank, danced and he had twice had sex with Jean. Eventually he decided to go home and suggested to the girl that she went with him but she said she was too tired and would rather stay where she was.

When he left, he said, Boshears was fairly sober and the girl was drowsy and 'pretty well asleep'.

The next witness was the American sergeant's wife who told how her husband went to ask Boshears to turn down his gramophone and how later, around 1.30 a.m. on New Year's morning, she heard what sounded like sobbing and the girl saying something like 'you don't love me'; it was muffled 'as though she was holding a handkerchief'.

So far straightforward stuff, the kind of evidence that is heard at murder trial after murder trial. The muffled sounds in the night, the lead up to the crime perhaps, thought the pressmen, writing busily. But then Detective Inspector Jeavons went into the box. He was a sturdy Essex man, around six feet tall and genuine as you would expect a policeman to be. In the dock Boshears sat in his smart uniform. Outside in the foyer Jean Boshears sat and smoked.

The first time the American told the Detective Inspector what happened it was a man making a pathetic attempt to try and prove that it was not he who was responsible for the death and the attempted cover-up.

'I saw him at the base,' Jeavons said, reading from his note book, 'and he said after caution "Jean and her boyfriend came round to my flat. It might have been after midnight. We had a few drinks in the living-room and I passed out.

"We were there an hour or two before that. I could not be sure. I don't know what time Jean and her boyfriend left." But he soon gave up his bravado and lying. A little while later he said to the inspector 'I may as well tell you the truth' and said he would make a statement.

He said that for some time they sat in the living-room and drank vodka and lemon squash 'for I don't know how long'. They were on a mattress and after a while the girl fell asleep. Boshears went on:

' "The other fellow and I had a couple more drinks and then I must have fell asleep – not asleep but passed out. The next thing I remember is the other fellow waking up and asking me where he could get a taxi." '

Nothing much there, just prelude to crime. Everyone in the court was waiting for what had happened, how he said it had happened. The inspector read from his note book methodically and carefully.

' "The next thing I remember was something pulling and scratching at my mouth. I opened my eyes and there was Jean lying under me and I had my hands round her throat. She was dead then. That sort of sobered me up. I got scared and did not know what to do.

' "I carried her body into the bedroom and put her clothes back on and left her lying on the floor." '

Yes? What next? Boshears went back to bed. Back to bed? Yes and slept. ' "When I woke up in the morning I decided it had been a dream." '

But when he looked in the bedroom he saw it was no dream but a nightmare and he was in the middle of it, wide awake with a corpse in the bed to bring in the New Year.

And there it lay for two days until 11.30 p.m. on 2

January when he carried the body downstairs wrapped in his heavy winter air force issue coat and laid it on the back seat of his car. He said he drove around and then put the body head first into a ditch. He burnt some of her clothes including her party dress, threw away her ring as he drove but still had her wristwatch and ten shillings, ten old shillings in a note. He took that from her purse.

He ended his statement to the inspector by saying 'I don't know what happened or why I did it.'

There was a pause as Mr Gerald Hines, defending the chirpy airman, got to his feet to ask whether it was right that Boshears and his wife were apart but only because of an arrangement following the birth of his son whereby she went to Scotland and that they were happily married and the wife was standing by him. Yes, said the inspector, that was right.

The next witness was the eminent pathologist, Dr Francis Camps. He was a man with an international reputation. The murders to which he had been called rate high in the list of any anthology of horrible crime. The most famous was John Reginald Halliday Christie who murdered at least six women at 10 Rillington Place; he also probably murdered the wife and child of his lodger, Timothy Evans, for which Evans was hanged and after a very long fight finally absolved of the murders, long after his death. Camps held the view that Christie, who was a necrophiliac sexually enjoying his victims as or after he gassed them to death, followed the pattern of mass murderers: once they have started killing they do not burn out but feed on the pleasure it gives them and have to go on and on. Christie was hanged.

Camps was called in when the body of motor dealer Stanley Setty was found in pieces and parcels on the Essex marshes and it was Camps who found that they had been dropped from an aircraft. Donald Hume was sent to prison for twelve years for accessory to the murder but when he came out of prison he sold his confession to murder to a Sunday paper before going off to Switzerland to murder three men, two bank guards and a taxi driver, during robberies and was sent to prison for life.

Camps had been involved in service murders before,

both involving 'the other woman'. One was the murder of one sergeant by another over the German wife of the victim in Germany. The other was Master Sergeant Marcus Marymont who was serving at RAF Sculthorpe in Norfolk when he decided to poison his wife with arsenic so he could marry his new girlfriend Cynthia. He gave his wife arsenic and to make sure he was doing the job well gave her a double dose just before her awful death.

When she was rushed to hospital he was asked by doctors, who were worried that she would not recover, for all the help he could give them. What earlier symptoms had there been, had she been ill like this before? They explained that she might die if they did not know what was wrong. But to their astonishment Marymont was casual, giving the impression that there was not much wrong with her and instead discussed his own personal problems with an emphasis on sex. After she had died as they had predicted he surprised them by asking 'what is a toxic liver?', certainly not the sort of question a husband who did not think his wife was seriously ill would be expected to ask. It made the doctors suspicious and they wanted an independent post-mortem and called in Camps.

Marymont was tried by US court martial, and the prosecutor, to test just how good this British guy was, asked how many post-mortems he had carried out. Camps paused, thinking, and then said, 'I should say at least 60,000.'

His evidence convicted Marymont who was jailed for thirty-five years. The woman he loved had lost interest before the trial because the American had told her that his wife had been long dead.

And now Camps was in the witness box again in an unusual case involving an American serviceman, this time in a British court where there was no one to query his credentials. But what did he think of Boshears's story that he had killed the girl as he slept?

Mr Rees asked 'On the findings which you made on the body did you think it is possible that he could have killed her while asleep in that way?'

Camps, a big, bluff and confident man, had considered

the point. He said 'I should think it is certainly within the bounds of improbability. My reason from my findings is this process would take a certain amount of time and during that period the person would go through certain phases of movement and from the description given of finding her suddenly dead like that I don't think it fits in with that type of death.'

Before he finished his evidence in chief, that is for the prosecution, and could be cross-examined on what was the key to the American's defence, the case was adjourned. When it was resumed Camps repeated what he had already said, that death was caused by manual strangulation with the pressure applied to the throat for about thirty seconds.

He was asked what effect that would have had on the girl. He said that she would have moved and that Boshears would have felt her moving even though he was half asleep.

The judge, Mr Justice Glyn-Jones, then joined in the questioning. 'He could not possibly have carried this through without waking himself up?'

Camps considered this. 'At least partially. There would also be the effect on the victim. If the victim was asleep she would also wake up. Everybody consciously protects themselves.'

That seemed to be the crux of his answer, his rebuttal, to the theory that the American did it in his sleep.

But it was not. Mr Hines suggested that the length of time pressure was applied was a matter for conjecture and the pathologist agreed that it was. He also agreed that bruises found on the body could well have been caused in moving after death.

There was only one witness for the defence and that was Boshears himself and the jury and everyone else in the court were eager to hear him give his version of his incredible dream.

He started by telling how he had spent New Year's Eve and it was a tale of drink and then more drink, first in the NCOs' club at the Wethersfield base. He planned to have a meal there and ordered bacon and eggs but could only eat one egg because he had just had a tooth out.

He set off home, stopping for a drink at Great Bardfield on the way and then having some vodka and lemonade in the flat before setting off at 5.30 p.m. to bring in the New Year. He drank his way round Braintree, mixing whisky and beer before returning to the Bell to see in the New Year; it was there, half an hour before midnight, that he met Jean and David.

They all went back to his flat where they drank in between the times the girl and her new boyfriend were having sex. Later the three of them lay down in front of the fire, Jean and David on the mattress, he on the floor. When David said he was going Boshears said he told him where to find a taxi.

The small American who spoke quietly but with the air of a man who had his story to tell and was not going to be diverted from the truth had finally reached the crunch in his evidence, the way that Jean had died. There was an expectancy in the court.

'When he had gone I sat down on the edge of the mattress,' he said, next to the sleeping girl.

'The next thing I remember,' he went on, 'was I felt something pulling at my mouth. I was not awake when I first felt it. It seemed to wake me up, I was over Jean and had my hands round her throat.'

There was complete silence in the court except for the soft American voice.

'Jean was dead. I panicked. I started to cut her hair off. Then I took the body to the spare bedroom and left it. I dressed her in the way in which she was later found. I took the sheets and blankets off the bed and put them in the bath tub to soak and went in and went to sleep.'

He meant the bed clothes from the matrimonial bed where Jean and David had had sex. Everyone knew that. But he was awake when he did all that. What did he do then, this man who had woken to find his hands round the neck of a girl?

'I had no idea of time. When I woke I decided it had been a dream. But when I found the body I was scared and shocked.'

So why did he take the body and dump it if he was asleep when she was killed? 'I am still not sure. I told lies to the police in the first instance because I was scared.'

It seemed reasonable. People do lie in panic when first approached by the police. It is very common and is acceptable if they tell the truth afterwards which Boshears had. Or had he? That was what the jury had to decide when they had heard all the evidence and it was not complete yet.

Mr Hines asked Boshears about his relationship to the girl. No, said Boshears, there had been no argument between them, he had not tried to have sex with her and he certainly had no desire to kill her.

Then it was the turn of the prosecution to test his story. Boshears told Mr Rees that he was sober when he took the body and dumped it in the ditch, when he threw the crumpled English rose so that her tarnished fingernails trailed in the wintry water of a stream under a wild rose bush.

But you were lying when you said you did not know why you did it, suggested Mr Rees. 'Yes, sir,' Boshears admitted.

'It is a lie because you knew exactly why you took the body to the ditch?' Mr Rees asked. Boshears did not disagree. 'Yes, sir,' he said quietly.

So Mr Rees pressed him further. Yes, Jean had been to the flat once before while his wife was up in Scotland. Nothing improper had happened, they had had a drink and she certainly did not stay the night and to show how proper it was he said his brother-in-law was there too.

He said that he had met Jean four or five times while his wife was away and always bought her drinks. There was nothing more to it than that.

Mr Rees then turned to the disposal of the body. He asked, 'In a sober and determined attempt to cover up what happened you carried her body into the bathroom and then into the bedroom. This was a calculated attempt to hide the crime you knew you had committed?'

'Yes sir.'

'What crime did you think you had committed?' Mr Rees moved in to the point.

'The logical one,' the American replied.

'But you didn't think it was a crime to kill someone

when you were fast asleep did you?' It was the key to everything. What answer could the American make to that except agree? But he did not answer the question directly.

'I thought to kill any way was a crime,' he said.

Whether that was right or wrong did not matter at that precise moment because the jury had an additional fact to consider about Boshears's explanation.

The pathologist had been recalled and asked about his view of strangling in one's sleep. He said:

'I would not go as far as to say it would be impossible.'

The judge just could not believe this. He looked at the pathologist incredulously and he was to make comments on it when he summed up the case to the jury a little later after the two closing speeches from the prosecution and the defence.

Mr Rees told the jury that they had to consider whether Boshears was lying or not about killing in his sleep. The prosecutor suggested that the American could not have been drunk because of what he did when he discovered the girl was dead. He suggested that what really happened was that once David had gone Boshears decided that he too would have sex and that when he tried there was trouble, the girl cried and 'she was hurt and he silenced her and she died.'

Mr Hines made the point that Boshears was asleep when David left and he could have easily fallen asleep again.

That left Mr Justice Glyn-Jones to sum up and from the start he made it clear to the jury that they had a choice of only two verdicts: guilty or not guilty of murder because the strangler put pressure on the girl's throat for such a length of time that he intended to cause death or grievous bodily harm which resulted in death. So the verdict had to be guilty of murder or nothing. There was no other offence. Manslaughter did not come into it. 'There is no lesser verdict open to you' the judge said. He went through the evidence and came to the defence.

By putting his hands round her neck for so long Boshears 'must have known the result of what he was doing'.

He went on, 'Have you ever heard of a man strangling a

woman while he was sound asleep? We have no medical evidence that there exists any record in all the records of the medical profession that such a thing has ever happened.

'But Dr Camps has said that it might be possible.'

'You use your commonsense and decide whether it happened.'

The judge obviously had his doubts. 'Is it within the bounds of possibility that Boshears could have moved from his position beside the girl on the mattress, removed the covering from her and then, straddling himself across her, caught her throat in his hands and applied pressure resulting in resistance, unconsciousness, convulsion and death, without being awakened by his own exertions?'

It was a matter for the jury. The judge was suggesting that they must use their ordinary commonsense to test whether the story made sense, was beyond reasonable doubt the answer to what had happened in front of the fire.

The jury went out and all those involved in the Boshears case went out too into the foyer to wait. Some went upstairs to the tea bar and sat in little groups discussing what the jury would decide, how long they would be out, whether they would be quick, whether they would take a long time, all the chitter-chatter that occurs when any jury retires to reach their verdict.

Jean Boshears went for a cup of tea and continued smoking. Down in the cells Boshears paced up and down, sat down, paced again, drank a cup of tea, then another.

In the court justice went on. A burglar from over the border in Cambridgeshire was in the dock, for justice does not stop when one case finishes and the jury goes out. The law is an extremely expensive commodity and when the public are paying by way of legal aid time is not wasted. The next case goes on until an usher who is in charge of the jury comes back and tells the clerk of the court that the jury are ready to return their verdict.

It was almost two hours before they were back. The clerk asked the foreman if they were all agreed upon their verdict and he said they were.

'Do you find the prisoner at the bar, Willis Eugene Boshears, guilty or not guilty of murder?'

'Not guilty.'

There was a loud gasp of astonishment and several people cried 'Why?' in sheer amazement. The judge looked bewildered and shook his head in disbelief.

A precedent had been set in British law. A defence could be run and succeed that a man, and thus theoretically a woman, could strangle in their sleep and it was no crime at all.

Boshears looked as baffled as everyone else. His counsel stood and asked if he could be released and the judge nodded. As Boshears stepped to freedom the court buzzed. The only people who did not seem concerned with the verdict were the jury of eleven men and one woman. They had created a talking point that would be discussed keenly for weeks and for years to come. It still is.

Outside the court while the necessary procedures were gone through before Boshears could walk free – like collecting his belongings and signing for them – his wife was spotted by the dead girl's mother who came over to speak to her.

'I feel very sorry for you,' Jean's mother Frances said with no bitterness. 'It must be terrible for you and the children.'

'Please believe me, I am sorry for you too,' Jean replied.

Then Jean, who had been too nervous, too apprehensive to go in and hear the verdict, was ushered away by reporters who had bought her story. She and her husband would have to wait to be reunited. A midnight tryst in an Essex hotel was planned.

She was quickly into a car and on the road. Her husband was not so lucky. He was in the middle of a tug-of-war on the steps of the court, a small figure with an enormous reporter from an American paper tugging one arm and an international swimmer, now a journalist on the paper who were paying good money for the little man's story, on the other. In the snow and lit by the flashes of the photographers Boshears was finally hurled into a car and driven off into a thick pea-souper fog.

When he and Jean finally were reunited they wept in each other's arms.

Jean said, 'I don't care about the weather, whether it is foggy or what. I have never been so happy. I forgive him.'

Boshears, who had been told he was a free man in the

United States Air Force and able to continue his career, spoke out freely.

'It sure was a relief to hear the foreman of that jury say those words "not guilty". I don't know yet whether I will be going back to the USA or not.

'But if I can I hope to forget about this whole tragic affair and settle down with my wife and family again.'

It was inevitably wishful thinking. He was not bothered by the press any more because the Americans battened down the hatches and no one is better at battening down hatches and hiding someone than the American Air Force. They were past masters at avoiding unpleasantness like that.

But the verdict aroused tremendous interest and nowhere more than in the House of Lords where it was discussed. It was a serious debate laced with a touch of ironic wit because no one could really accept that it had happened. The cries of 'why?' that came out as a natural reaction in the courtroom were echoed around the country.

It was Lord Elton who raised the matter. He asked the government – the prime minister was Harold Macmillan – whether as a result of the acquittal of a defendant in a recent murder trial on the ground he was asleep they were considering bringing about a change in the law to make possible a verdict of 'guilty but asleep'.

Earl Bathurst, under secretary at the Home Office, had no doubts. He said: 'From the inquiries I have been able to make it would appear that the circumstances of this case are without precedent. I have no reason to think that it has demonstrated the need for a change in the law.'

Lord Elton was not satisfied. He retorted, 'Would not the under secretary agree that a verdict of "guilty but asleep" would be much nearer to the facts than a verdict of innocent and would also have the advantage that like a verdict of "guilty but insane" it would make it possible to detain the convicted person?

'Would not he agree that when a bizarre case like this has been widely reported it is more than likely that it will be imitated subconsciously and half-wittingly by persons of neurotic temperament or deliberately simulated by persons who desire a plausible line of defence?'

He had a point. Earl Bathurst replied, 'It is true that there might be a possibility that the verdict of "asleep" might in future be considered to be part of mental disorder and the Home Secretary is looking into that very carefully.

'Meanwhile I can only say that so far as this is an extraordinary result of a case, such an extraordinary decision has been made, that for the time being the Home Secretary sees no reason to alter the law.'

Not all the Lords in the House were happy. Lord Amwell was puzzled.

'If a man is asleep how can he be guilty?' he asked and everyone had a good laugh.

'Oh, no,' declared Lord Derwent. 'Surely the man was not guilty? He was found not guilty.'

Earl Bathurst came in again. 'That is right. The point Lord Amwell brought up is the conundrum we are faced with.'

In came Lord Ogmore. He had a legal point.

'Is it proper for a minister of the Crown to describe the verdict and decision in a case as extraordinary?'

It was a question that needed a legal brain to answer and up stood Viscount Hailsham, later, much later to become Lord Hailsham and Lord Chancellor, but then leader of the House. He knew the answer. He said:

'I think my noble friend meant to say, as in his original answer, that it was wholly without precedent. In that sense I think it is not improper.'

Lord Ogmore was not having it. He said, 'In the sense that the words were used by the minister they were improper.'

But Viscount Hailsham stood firm. 'I am sure that my noble friend did not wish to question the verdict of the court in any way.'

And then to end the short debate Lady Summerskill asked Viscount Hailsham in his role as leader of the House if he did not agree that precedent played a most important part in the law.

Ah, said Viscount Hailsham, there was a difference. The verdict of a jury was not a precedent in the legal sense. A legal precedent was a decision by a judge.

There it was left by the Lords.

The Home Secretary, however carefully he considered the matter, never did give a pungent decision that could have changed the law. It stayed just as it was and although one or two hopefuls put up a defence that they were asleep they were quickly knocked down by their legal advisers or the courts.

Boshears went into hospital for a check-up and the American doctors pronounced him quite fit, normal and sane. He and his wife celebrated over a candlelit dinner as they talked through the whole sorry story.

Early in March Boshears was transferred back to the States to a base at Glasgow, Montana. By that time he had had leave and the American Air Force had paid him his back pay of 800 dollars accumulated while he was in prison awaiting trial.

But back in the States the air force had second thoughts and the staff sergeant was told his services were no longer required. A spokesman for USAF said that he had been dismissed 'under other than honourable conditions' but would not elaborate. 'There is no explanation,' he said.

Boshears went into civilian life. But like Jean Constable's life his ended tragically too.

No one was asleep at the time. He died in a car crash.

2

The Barn

A Case of Identity

At two o'clock in the morning of Guy Fawkes Day 1972 the Barn restaurant at Braintree was bouncing. The 350 guests who had paid £5 a head for a good night out with dinner, dancing and a cabaret inside and a firework display outside were still enjoying themselves in an old English-style restaurant. Outside the neon sign announced, 'Every night is party night.'

It was true. In the ten years since bouncy, perky Bob Patience, an astute self-made East Ender, who had been a wartime RAF air-gunner, and his wife Muriel had bought the modest tea rooms on the Braintree–Great Dunmow road, they had turned it into a booming nightspot for customers from east London, Essex and the eastern counties.

Bob, always dapper and welcoming in his familiar white dinner jacket, was a magnificent host and ran his family business – son David, now twenty-three and daughter Beverley, twenty, joined in as they grew up – with flair.

Some of his customers were on the fringes of crime. He knew about that area from a former nightspot, the Ranch House which he ran – with a wild-west image – in Ilford. It was another boom business for the former firewood and log salesman. But the gangland war was on in the East End in those days and shortly before Christmas 1960 a young customer was involved in a fracas in which Bob was punched on the nose. Then the customer was taken outside and in the fight died. The four men accused of killing him were later acquitted but before then Bob was taken for a ride, American-style, after being ordered into a car which stopped beside him on his way from home to the club on a Sunday morning.

He was driven to an engineering firm in nearby Chadwell Heath where he was told in no uncertain terms by men whom police believe were members of the notorious Kray twins' team (they are still inside for two murders), that some members of his club were potential witnesses to the killing. As owner of the club he should contact them and tell them that 'bad memories would be advisable'.

To emphasize the point one of the men went to the window, opened it, drew a gun from his coat and shot out of the window. 'Tell them it only barks once,' he said. Then Bob was driven home.

But that November early morning twelve years later Bob had no worries as he took one last look at the long, high-beamed dining-room where his happy customers enjoyed themselves in the country hospitality atmosphere of antiques, brass and bric-à-brac which he cultivated. 'Where countryside hospitality bids you' one sign outside invited the customers in.

Bob went back to his office to finish counting the takings. His blonde wife, aged fifty-one, and daughter Beverley had gone over to the family's four-bedroom house, Sun Lido, fifteen minutes earlier, tired after the hard evening.

Bob told David, the restaurant manager, to close up when the guests went, and walked the short distance over the gravel car-park to the house.

What he found as he opened the front door was to start one of the most fantastic murder cases of the decade, involving questions of identity and bullion robbery; rumour, innuendo and accusation; and East London gangland and gunmen.

Fifteen minutes earlier Beverley had swung open the front door to come face to face in the hallway with a man holding a pistol in his hand and pointing it at her. As she screamed a second man came out of the kitchen. Neither had made any attempt to disguise their appearance. Beverley instinctively stepped back into her mother's path.

The gunman waved his pistol and snapped, 'Be quiet, it's not you we want,' and ushered them into the lounge and made them sit on the settee. Beverley tried to comfort her mother who was nearly hysterical. They were told again by the gunman to be quiet.

He took a cushion and held it across the muzzle of his gun saying, 'Be quiet because if I have to use it, it won't make any noise.'

The second man said nothing. The only thing he did was to go into the kitchen to get a glass of water for Muriel.

The gunman then asked them where the key to the safe was. The women said it was in the restaurant. Beverley thought from his accent that he was from the north, Yorkshire perhaps.

Outside people were leaving the restaurant in merry mood, slamming car doors, laughing, revving their engines.

Then Bob came in. As he came through the door his wife cried out, 'Don't do anything, Bob, they've got a gun' and as she spoke he found he was looking down the barrel of a Beretta automatic pistol.

He was ordered to sit down and hand over the keys of the safe. Bob tried bluff, saying they were over in the restaurant although they had actually been on the table in the lounge all the time. He tried another bluff by saying there was no money in the safe anyway and then tried bargaining, offering to get the key in exchange for no harm coming to his wife and daughter.

The gunman became angry and called Bob by his Christian name, explaining he knew this in the same way he knew about the restaurant and the money in the safe.

The situation became tense as he demanded the key and Bob insisted he did not have it.

Then, to the three's absolute, horrified amazement, the gunman nuzzled the pistol into the cushion and pointed it at the two women.

He said slowly, 'This is a family affair,' and began swinging the gun between the two women as if deciding between them. 'Your wife or your daughter,' he muttered and then, 'Your wife I think.'

There was a muffled bang and feathers flew as the gun went off and Muriel cried out as the bullet went into her forehead.

It was so unexpected, so appalling, that for a second there was silence. The gunman broke it. Without emotion or any sign of what he had done he demanded the key for the safe, waving Bob back with the gun as he tried to go to his wife's aid.

He went into the hall, opened the safe and took out two bank bags containing the takings from the restaurant, about £2,000 in cheques and credit card slips but only £900 in cash.

The gunman seemed satisfied and they went back into the lounge. Bob, the cool man even in such circumstances, had left £7,300 in cash and his wife's jewels in the safe.

The gunman inspected the unconscious Muriel and said, 'She'll be all right. I've seen plenty of these in my time,' and ignored the pleas of Bob and Beverley to get an ambulance.

Instead he told his accomplice who had not said a word to get something with which to tie father and daughter. He did, bringing back a blue plastic clothes line and some ties and also a towel to stop the bleeding from Muriel's head.

Father and daughter were ordered to lie face down on the floor and were bound hand and foot and both gagged, the girl with tights, the father with one of his ties.

But instead of going as his accomplice did, the gunman stayed to execute them in cold blood, undoubtedly to make sure that they would never live to identify the two robbers.

Beverley's heart stopped as she saw the gunman walk across to her. She tried to scream but was trussed like a ceremonial pig. She felt the man kneel over her, put the cushion on her back, push the gun into it and fire.

She screamed and then fell.

Bob lay there in terror for his daughter, for himself, impotent to do anything but wait his turn in his lounge in his home in the quiet Essex countryside, not like the wild west that he had seen on his visit to America.

The man with the gun did not hesitate. As if swatting a

fly he put the cushion on Bob's left ear, pressed the gun into it and fired. The restaurateur flopped face first onto the ground.

The gunman took one last look, picked up some car keys from the table and calmly walked out to join his accomplice in the car-park, the executioner satisfied that the evidence had gone forever.

Incredibly, he was wrong. A few minutes after the robbers had gone in David's blue fast-back Volkswagen with the keys they had taken, Bob came round. The bullet had hit a bone in his ear and instead of ploughing into his brain to kill him, had bounced off. He was deaf and shocked for several days but otherwise all right.

Beverley recovered too. She was seriously ill for some time because the bullet had entered her back, passed right through her body missing the aorta artery by only a quarter of an inch – it would have been instant death if it had hit – and come out through her stomach.

Her mother was less lucky. An X-ray showed the bullet lodged deep in the back of the brain; she remained unconscious until 8 November when she started respiratory problems and died.

It was now a case of murder and as soon as it became one on 8 November the police had to wait only a day before a name was whispered over the phone to them from the East End.

The caller said, 'The man you want is George Henry Ince.'

The trouble that call was to cause and the motives of the man who made it led to fifteen months of headline-making news stories.

By the time the police received the call four days had passed since Bob, once he had opened his eyes and realized that he was alive, had called his son David, twenty-three, on the intercom and raised the alarm. As David ran to the house he saw his VW being driven away but he did not stop it, thinking it might be someone on their way to get help. It turned up six hours later in a field six miles away, found by a retired shepherd down a chalk farm track in the middle of a sugar beet field. Dozens of policemen with dogs spent hours and days searching the area, the fields and hedgerows for some clue to the two men who had abandoned the car but without any luck at all. It was as if they had vanished into thin air.

Police knew what they looked like for Bob and Beverley were able to give very good descriptions. The callous gunman was said to be about thirty, five foot nine inches tall with a northern accent. He had blue eyes, sandy blond receding hair and a thin face with sallow complexion. His accomplice, the quiet, non-violent one of the pair, was nearer six feet tall, slim with brown eyes and in his late twenties.

George Ince looked like the gunman and like the photofit picture that was built up with Bob and Beverley's aid with points of alteration to make the likeness as perfect as they could remember.

Police too had a description of two strangers who could well have been the robbers from the landlord of a pub in nearby Felsted who remembered them being there on the Thursday before the shootings, and also from a retired policeman who said he had been asked the way to the road in which the Barn stood twelve hours before the crime by two men. One, he particularly noticed, had something wrong with his right eye, a cast or lazy eye, which he recalled vividly, and the other man seemed more intelligent and a more pleasant personality than the first. It was something that became important later.

But at that stage police were after Ince. They already had him on their files as a suspect in a daring £400,000 silver bullion hijack in May 1972, six months before the murder. It was a robbery carried out with the audacity of an old-fashioned highway robbery with military precision and would have netted the gang much more than the 99 ingots worth around £60,000 that they had time to take away, had a milkman not held them up; after they had snatched the bullion lorry on its way to Harwich down the A12 from London at the Essex village of Mountnessing, he drove his float zig-zag across them as they made the exchange.

He carried on to the police station and the robbers heard via police wavelengths they could pick up on their transistors that they had to get away quickly. They left nearly 550 ingots behind. Ince was thought to be one of the team.

There was another reason why police knew a lot about Ince, once a minor criminal whose last conviction was eleven years before.

He was in love with Charlie Kray's wife, Dolly, and after a long courtship they had become lovers. It was a romance fraught with danger. Charlie, older than the terrible twins whose reign of terror in the East End was terrifying to those who crossed their paths, heard of what was going on and called Ince to see him. He went, there was a talk and the young cockney was advised to leave Dolly alone. He did not take that advice.

A few years later the Krays' gangland hold was smashed and the twins went to jail for life with a recommendation that they served a minimum of thirty years for murder. Mr Justice Melford Stevenson said he thought it was time that the public had a rest from their activities. Charlie Kray was jailed for ten years for being an accessory to the murder of Jack the Hat McVitie, a renegade gang member who was stabbed to death as he was held.

The cat was away and the mouse had the field to himself in which to play. Dolly changed her name to Gray and a year after her husband had been jailed she and George became lovers.

But just because a person is in prison it does not mean that he has not friends on the outside; Charlie Kray's friends decided that young Ince should be taught a lesson on behalf of the unknowing friend languishing in a cell. One night George arrived back at his flat to find some men waiting for him outside the door on the seventh floor. They clubbed, punched and kicked him and then systematically broke every finger on each hand before one of the men pulled a gun and shot him in the calf of his right leg. When police arrived he said he had not been attacked but fallen from a building. The police did not press him too much. They knew he would not change his story. It was the law of the jungle and men like Ince lived in a kind of a jungle.

A year later an attempt was made to deter true love

running smoothly again. As George was walking home at night a car stopped, he was dragged inside and beaten. Then a twelve-bore shotgun was thrust down the waist of his trousers and the gunman grinned and pulled the trigger. The shot missed the vital part and tore into the muscle of his leg. The attackers dropped him outside a hospital, pushing him out onto the pavement.

It was just an accident, Ince told the police.

And that was not the end of the efforts to stop him seeing Dolly who was just as much in love with George as he with her. She knew the rules of the jungle too and was worried but love, as the wise say, conquers all.

George was coming out of an East End pub after a drink with a friend when a passing car veered towards them and from a window a gun poked out Chicago Al Capone-style and a shot thudded into George's VW. It did not stop the Romeo but he did move out of town and down to the Kent coast, not as police were later to suggest, because he was wanted for the silver bullion robbery, but because he wanted to avoid being involved as a witness in another gangland case that had been busted.

George had been warned in a pub by a man whose threats he took seriously (and who ironically was to be shot dead in a domestic triangle) that if he was called as a witness and said who shot him he would be a dead man. George took that threat seriously and went to live in a caravan at Whitstable.

This was the man who was now 'in the frame' as the callous gunman who had killed one woman and tried to murder her husband and daughter so that they would not be able to give evidence against him. Over one hundred Essex policemen, some armed, were out looking for him and other forces joined in. His flat, his relatives and friends, his haunts were visited.

And so was Dolly Gray. She could not help.

Her lover knew that he was wanted but he was not worried. Apart from the fact that he was innocent he also had an alibi. The night of the murder, Guy Fawkes night, he was with Dolly and they had slept together and he had a statement from her saying that that was so.

He decided to give himself up, show the police the alibi,

let them check it out and then he would be cleared from the inquiry.

But by the time he did so with his solicitor on 27 November at Epping police station, later telling police that he chose it because it was the first police station in Essex and did not want to take the chance of being shot, two important things had happened:

Beverley in her hospital bed was shown many photographs of different men in a photographic identity parade. She picked out Ince but said that he should be thinner in the face and have blue eyes. Later she was shown other pictures of Ince and other men and again she picked his out and said, 'If this man has blue eyes I'm positive.'

Later she was shown a snapshot of Ince and this time she could see his eyes were blue. 'Yes, that's him, I'm sure,' she said.

The other point involved Dolly. She was seen by Essex police and although she admitted that she had known him she said she had not seen him for years.

George countered this when he was first interviewed after giving himself up by saying: 'Well she never wanted to tell the police I was having an affair with her, that's all I can say.'

But by this time he suddenly realized that a net was tightening round him. Whoever had tipped off the police – again possibly someone who did not like his affair with Dolly – must have been sitting back and laughing. It was working wonderfully well and it became worse when George was put on an identity parade at Colchester police station.

Bob Patience picked him out after some doubts over whether he was the man, which position he was standing in, what coloured shirt he was wearing – George had switched shirts with his solicitor before the parade – but son David had no doubts that Ince was the man he had seen in the passenger seat of his VW being driven out of the car-park as he answered his father's call for help.

But far worse was when Beverley came to look at the twelve men – eleven off the street as volunteers and George, all looking roughly the same. She only walked past five, stopped, turned and walked back to George who was third in the line and touched him on the shoulder.

His troubles did not end there. He had been so shocked when he was picked out that he wanted to shout out that it was not him but the words would not come. As police went on looking for the second man, he was charged, appeared in court at Braintree and then went on another identity parade where one of the customers at the pub in Felsted said that he thought George was one of the two men he had seen there before the murder.

Eventually, still protesting his innocence, he was committed to stand his trial at Chelmsford (having also been committed for trial for his part in the silver bullion robbery to the Old Bailey, a crime he also denied). Before the trial could take place another possible nail was banged firmly into place against him.

Scotland Yard scientific officer Margaret Pereira had been examining George's clothes and on his overcoat she found two turquoise acrylic fibres which matched in every detail the German-manufactured material covering the suite in the Patiences' living-room at the Barn. It was not conclusive but tied in with the identification by five people – and George only had Dolly to say he was not there and he was not willing to call her after she had already told the police he had not been with her. The inference was that he was at the Barn and he was the killer.

It was extremely worrying and he had that worry until the trial when his defence team, using their own scientific officer, discovered that his sister Rosie had owned a suite of furniture which was covered in the same material as that in Sun Lido House and that she had given it to a neighbour, but after the police had collected George's overcoat from her home. The fibres could easily have come from Rosie's material when the coat was laid upon it. It was a great relief to George; the case revolved round his identification by the five witnesses and nothing else. There was no other scientific evidence.

The trial began on Wednesday 2 May 1973 before Mr Justice Melford Stevenson. He was still presiding despite a plea from the defence that the case should be heard before another judge. Stevenson turned it down. George was worried about the judge who had a reputation for severity, for a very good reason: he had jailed his lover's husband for ten years when dealing with the Kray gang.

George pleaded not guilty to the six charges of murder, attempted murder or alternatively wounding them and stealing the money.

Mr John Leonard QC, prosecuting, outlined the facts to the jury and then called Bob Patience. He told how he walked into Sun Lido House that Guy Fawkes morning, past Kipper the dog and straight into the sights of a man with a gun and that man – and he had no doubt – was the man in the dock, George Ince.

And the man who made repeated demands for the money was the same man, the man who shot his wife.

George could not contain himself. He leapt up and shouted, 'Why don't you tell the truth? You know I wasn't the one that done it.'

Bob said, 'I am telling the truth.'

Then he told how his plea for help for his wife was ignored, how first his daughter then he were shot.

He was then asked about the identification parade and he told how he became muddled and picked the wrong person, realized he had made a mistake and then named George Ince. He was cross-examined by Mr Victor Durand QC for Ince, over the identification and how he was mistaken. It was a question of the colour of the shirt George was wearing, he explained. Later the colour of the shirt, whether it was green or not, was a much more important point in the trial.

Bob was followed by Beverley who told the same harrowing, horrific story of what had happened in the early hours. When it was her turn for execution, she said, 'He put a cushion over my back and then shot me. I had my head turned to the left and I could see. The gun went into the cushion. I screamed, "No, don't". Then he fired.'

She said she had picked out George at the identity parade but during cross-examination over the photographs she had seen, George leapt forward and shouted, 'Why don't you tell the truth?' and Beverley dissolved into tears and was led from the court sobbing. The court was adjourned for a short time and when reconvened the judge ordered that George be taken down to the cells while Beverley finished her evidence in case there was another outburst.

It was the beginning of an extraordinary set of events that went on until the jury came back after considering their verdict.

More evidence was given identifying George as being in Felsted and the area, all of which he denied. On the fifth day of the trial he had had enough. His anger and frustration, all the hatred and despair he had felt since he went to give himself up knowing that he was innocent and could prove it, bursting like a great boil. For three hours he discussed the situation with his legal team and then appeared in the dock to ask for another judge and accused Stevenson of being biased and rude. George's legal team refused to be associated with his views and the judge said he was not stopping the trial. An accused person could challenge the jury but not the judge.

Down the stairs to the cells George and his legal team disappeared again only for Mr Durand to reappear and say that George did not want them to appear for him any more, a decision explained by George who told the judge he wanted them to represent him but 'not in this court – not in front of you'.

George then headed for the cells again but was stopped on the judge's orders. He was told that George wanted no further part of the trial and he did not want the judge to hear the case, but when the judge insisted that he remained, the little cockney made his final and supreme gesture. He turned his back on the judge and stayed that way for the rest of the trial.

He called no defence, had his request for a truth-drug test turned down and made remarks as the judge summed up the case for the jury who finally retired to consider their verdict. They were a long time doing so and over three hours had passed before the judge recalled them to tell them they could now return a majority verdict of at least ten for a verdict although he would prefer a unanimous decision. Off they went again but thirty-five minutes later they were back and the foreman handed the judge a note. It said that they were divided nine to three and they were finding it difficult to reach a decision because Ince had not called any evidence. The judge sympathized with them but repeated it had to be ten to two, no less. As they went out again George shouted at the judge: 'May God forgive you, sir, because I did not do this.'

Six and a half hours after they had first left the court to consider their decision they came back. It was twenty-five minutes past nine at night and everyone involved in the case was tired and emotionally drained.

The clerk of the court asked the foreman whether at least ten of them had agreed upon a verdict on the first charge, the one of murder. 'No,' said the foreman, a word he repeated five more times as the other charges were put to him.

The judge listened and then said, 'There it is, gentlemen. It is perfectly obvious you tried your best and in these circumstances the whole case will have to be tried again which, of course, is a profound public misfortune and a profound private misfortune for those involved. But there is nothing else one can do about it and I can only discharge you.'

George turned to the jury and said, 'I would like to thank the members of the jury for giving me a chance to let my case go forward before a truthful judge and not a biased judge.'

He was taken to the cells and everyone else went home.

He was a very lucky man. The nine–three balance the judge was told about was in favour of convicting him. Only one man stood between him and a guilty verdict and a mandatory sentence of life imprisonment.

The jury's verdict meant a retrial. Often there can be a gap of several weeks before it takes place but in George's case there was a gap of only a few days. The new trial started on the following Monday in front of another judge, Mr Justice Eveleigh, a big man in every way. He sat in one court and in the next one Melford Stevenson listened to another murder, that by an escaped prisoner from Wormwood Scrubs jail who had taken lodgings in Hertfordshire, fallen in love with his landlady who did not like her husband, and killed him. The wife went up to watch her lover dispose of the body by fire, saying she had always wanted to see her husband burn in hell. The lover was eventually found guilty and was led weeping to the cells to start a life sentence. It was interesting in view of George Ince's opinion of the judge that one of the jurymen said after the trial of the escaped prisoner that the jury had stayed out longer than was necessary on the evidence because they did not like the judge's attitude.

However in George's case the retrial ran more smoothly. Bob Patience was again first witness after the prosecution had outlined the facts, telling the jury that they would have had to be deaf or blind not to have known what happened at the first trial. Bob, looking tired and drawn, went into the witness box and said, as firmly as before, that the man in the dock was the same man who had shot his wife.

Again the question of the identity parade came up; had Bob seen pictures of George before, how many, was he connected with the silver bullion robbery, was he sure?

Bob put it quite clearly after a lot of questions. 'At the committal proceedings before the magistrates Ince jumped up shouting. I was sitting in direct line with him and if he had had a gun in his hand he would have been identical with the man who shot my wife that night, the same voice and the same tense and white features. That is the man, without a doubt, who shot my wife, shot me and shot my daughter.

'Voices do come into it, sir. I also heard him last week or the week before in this very court when he accused me of not telling the truth – the same voice, the same man who has got an uncontrollable temper. There he is ... there,' and he pointed to the dock.

Beverley followed her father and again identified George as the man who had shot her. Again the questioning was on the lines of whether she had seen photographs before the identity parade or afterwards.

As the trial went on the identity parade and when George had changed his shirt became of vital importance. It hinged on whether it had happened before Bob walked up and down the parade and where George stood and just how many times George did change his shirt, whether it was once, twice or three times. For the case now hinged entirely on identification. There was no scientific evidence to link George with the Barn at all.

He gave evidence for the first time and denied absolutely that he had anything to do with it, had never been to the Barn and did not know the family and never had.

On the night of the murder he was at the flat – and he was allowed to write down the address – of Mrs Gray. Once her little girl had gone to bed he and Mrs Gray watched television until after midnight and then went to bed and did not get up until about quarter to eight and two hours later he went back to Whitstable.

When he was cross-examined George said, 'I honestly say, I honestly think they have made a terrible mistake, sir. I am completely innocent.'

Then there was talk about Mrs Gray and her real name in case, if she used a pseudonym, people might contradict her evidence. It was left in abeyance as George told how it was his practice to stay every Saturday night with Mrs Gray who had changed her name by deed poll in 1969. Their relationship had lasted three and a half years. When the judge asked the strength of the relationship, George said they were in love.

The week ended after five days of evidence and for George it was a worrying weekend because he knew he had to involve Dolly publicly much as he did not want to do so. But he and his legal team knew there was no other choice if he was to be freed.

On Monday fair-haired Dolly took all her courage in her hands and walked into the witness box to help the man she loved. Tall and slim she stood nervously before she was allowed to sit down. The code of the East End jungle was being broken and she had every right to feel shaky and apprehensive. She knew how the people she had spent her life with were likely to react.

She said they had known each other for fourteen, fifteen years but in the last five years they had become intimate. On the night of the murder he was beside her in bed all night and he could not have left the room.

She said as far as she knew her husband did not know

of her involvement but she did not make it clear whether that meant her involvement in the trial or with the man in the dock. When she was cross-examined she said that her husband was not about at the moment and had not been since the start of 1969 and he knew that she had changed her name by deed poll.

The jury were given the odd clue as to her real name by references to some questions one of the Essex detectives had asked when checking George's original alibi. She had said that George used to go to her two brothers-in-law's billiards hall in Mile End and by that she meant the brothers of her husband.

She had been quite steady but the pressure was beginning to tell. She said:

'The only question Mr May [the Essex detective] asked was whether I knew George Ince and I said I had for fourteen or fifteen years. I am telling the absolute truth.

'I have not come here to lie. I have got my home and my family to lose.'

She became emotional when she was accused of coming to court to give George a false alibi. Shaking, she declared:

'I am telling the absolute truth. This man never left my side when he came on the Saturday and left on the Sunday. I would like you to bear in mind the publicity I am getting. I stand to lose my home and family but I have come here to tell the absolute truth.

'I am a Catholic and I will not come here to lie.'

When she left the court George turned towards her, holding an outstretched cross in his hands. She did not look but walked straight out through the swing doors.

It then turned out that the prosecutor by mistake had called her Mrs Kray. Had the jury heard it or had the judge's quick interruption by talking, taken the edge off what might have been a difficult situation? That it was a slip of the tongue there was no doubt but it was, everyone agreed, most unfortunate.

The press who had heard – and most knew anyway – were asked not to refer to the slip nor to her real identity and they all complied.

The closing speeches were brief, dramatic and very much to the point. Mr Victor Durand, QC, defending, said that the most spectacular miscarriages of justice had been due to the wrong identification of an accused man. Was there not a risk in this case that Ince's face was familiar unintentionally to those who would later be called as witnesses because they had seen his photograph?

Much of his case rested on Dolly Gray's evidence that George was with her all night. Mr Durand put it this way:

'Was that woman acting yesterday? If you think she may be right this prisoner Ince, however worthless he may be in your estimation, is entitled to say to twelve Englishmen, "You cannot find me guilty." '

The defending barrister challenged the suggestion by the prosecution that George had left Dolly to carry out the raid. He said:

'Is the suggestion to be left that in this night there was just one single lingering melt of these two, a short night of lust? Or may it be that this woman is right? That she, the satisfied woman, goes on in delight with this man, his body in her possession until the danger of the son coming home next day.'

On Wednesday 23 May the jury retired at lunchtime. During the wait a letter arrived, addressed to defence counsel and postmarked Wisbech, Cambridgeshire, purporting to be from the killer. It turned out later to be nothing but a hoax.

Three hours six minutes after they had gone out the jury returned. When they announced that George was not guilty of murder there was uproar. That meant that all the other verdicts would be not guilty.

When those had been returned, once the judge had restored order by threatening to clear the court, George could not hold back his fury. Six months and two trials had imposed a terrible strain on him and he pointed at the detectives, screaming:

'Now it's your turn for the corruption.' And as he was led to the cells, for he was still on remand in custody for the silver bullion robbery and awaiting trial for that (he received fifteen years for his part in it), he roared:

'You are all corrupt. Tell them about the fucking money you had.'

After the case Dolly was identified to the world in the

papers as Mrs Dolly Kray, wife of Charlie. She had risked everything to save her lover and her honesty and guts had won the day. She had to go home alone, to her 21-year-old son and seven-year-old daughter but she could hold her head high and accept that she was no longer one of the crowd with whom she had grown up.

'We are in love,' she had said and it was right. Her love had conquered fear, everything.

The police walked away, some convinced that George Henry Ince had indeed got away with murder. Others were baffled. All their inquiries were pointed at George and as they explained it was not their decision that finally decided on prosecution but that of the Director of Public Prosecutions who studied the file they had compiled and said they should go ahead, charge George and let a jury decide. That was what had happened.

But it left questions unresolved. What about the second man? He had not been found but had the killer murdered him also so that he could tell no tales? It was a theory that might well fit the facts, because of him there was not a trace.

And if George Henry Ince was not the murderer – and he had most emphatically been cleared by a jury – then who on earth had broken into the Barn that November night and committed murder most foul?

The answer came less than a month later.

While George Ince was languishing in jail, not knowing whether he was going to be sentenced to life imprisonment for a murder he insisted – and later it was to be proved – that he did not commit, another man was telling those who listened when he had had a few drinks that he owned the gun which shot the Patience family.

His name was John Brook, two years younger than George, and not only had he shown off the Beretta but had fired three shots in and around the Ambleside hotel in the Lake District where he had been taken on as a kitchen porter.

The information came out of the blue, 300 miles from the Barn, from a petty thief with a criminal record who gave himself up to police at Kendal, knowing they were looking for him for a car-wash break-in. While he was admitting what he had done he told them about a man he had worked with a few weeks earlier at an Ambleside hotel who carried a pistol tucked in the waistband of his trousers.

Police traced Brook to a restaurant in Bowness-on-Windermere and shortly after went to his room at the hotel at Ambleside from which he had since moved. They found a split under his mattress, suggesting that he had hidden the gun he now denied owning there. They went to his new lodgings, turned over the mattress and there tucked in it was the .32 Beretta.

Brook told them several stories but eventually said that he had arranged to buy it while serving a sentence in Dartmoor and it cost him £100. It was delivered shortly after he was released. He got seventeen rounds with the pistol, he said, and he had fired three of them.

Police checked his record and found that it was bad and also indicated that he had no regard for human life. The conviction that had put him in Dartmoor was for beating a friend with an iron bar.

Essex police were immediately told and the gun sent for forensic examination. Tests showed that the gun was the one used to kill Mrs Patience and shoot her husband and daughter.

Essex police did not move until the results were known. They were worried that it might be a red herring. They had already handed back some of the exhibits to Bob Patience and those he did not want had been thrown on to the rubbish dump.

But once the confirmation that the Beretta was the gun came through, Detective Chief Superintendent Len White, then head of Essex CID, who had been in charge of the murder from the very start and had lived it day after day, carrying the immense burden that the case had already thrown up, went up to the Lake District to see this man Brook and find out whether or not he was the murderer.

The first thing that struck White and his colleagues and struck them forcibly, was the fact that he fitted the general description of the killer and even more, he had a glass right eye which gave him the staring appearance that both Beverley and a retired police officer had mentioned.

They realized only too clearly that George Ince could have been the victim of a classic case of mistaken identity. But if Brook was in the frame, who on earth was his number two, the man who had tied up the Patiences, the man who did not use a gun, the man they had not been able to trace?

Brook said from the start he was not the man. The thief in custody might have said that he had admitted it but that was not true. He had been in Leeds at his grandmother's on the night of the shooting.

Perhaps someone else had used his gun to do the shooting because if it had been him he would have thrown it away; that was commonsense, he explained.

By that time, Brook had been up in court and remanded at Kendal for unlawful possession of the pistol and the ammunition. He was remanded again while White and his team considered the possibilities and the evidence.

They knew that it was Brook's gun but there was no evidence that it was his finger that pulled the trigger. They needed to find the accomplice. They did what they should have done earlier if they had not been so certain that George Ince was their man. They had thought his accomplice would be one of his criminal acquaintances, perhaps one of the men in the silver bullion raid, or someone missing and dead, but they never got near to him. Now they had a new suspect and they were growing more and more certain that he was the killer. Not just because it was his gun that was used but from his appearance. They had to find the second man.

It was a piece of one routine but deadly dull police work which often goes unsung but is vital in so many inquiries, that finally produced a man who could well have been Brook's accomplice.

They checked on every person who had shared a cell with Brook during the many times he had been in custody. One name came out as favourite: Nicholas Michael de Clare Johnson, aged thirty, a small-time con man with no history of anything like the Barn murder. But he looked like the description of the second man and in his make-up was a kindly streak which fitted into the pattern of showing more sympathy to the Patiences while the killer was behaving without thought for life.

He had been in Grendon Underwood psychiatric hospital at the same time as Brook and was with Brook on the pre-release hostel system in London. The records showed that he was still serving a sentence at the time of the murder but had booked out for weekend leave with a man who became a father to him, in Romsey, Hampshire.

Now he was back in jail again, on remand awaiting trial for stealing a wallet and car from his benefactor who had since died.

Luckily, he had kept a diary and it showed that Johnson did not turn up at Romsey until the Sunday of the Guy Fawkes weekend, the day after the killing.

Chief Superintendent White and his deputy, Detective Superintendent George Harris, who like his superior had been involved throughout the case, went to see Johnson, who could be fairly described as an all-round loser, illegitimate, inept, articulate and pleasant but always finding the worst company. His friendship with hard man Brook was typical of his life-style and so was robbing the man who had befriended him. Even the courts recognized his as a social problem rather than a criminal one.

The two Essex policemen saw him a few hours after he had been sentenced to fifteen months' imprisonment for stealing from his benefactor. They used kid-glove tactics to interview him and draw from him gradually and gently just what had happened. The interview took some time and was text-book style in its brilliant use of fair and genuine police interrogation tactics.

Finally, Johnson who had hedged and really told them nothing began to crack up. It was when Harris mentioned the kindness to the Patiences that Johnson said:

'I have been suffering from migraine and violent stomach pains from about that time.' Then he said, 'Just charge me. I have had it on my memory for a long time. I haven't been to church since.'

Then he added, 'Why do you think I got hepatitis?' The words began to come out in a trickle. 'I am ashamed of what happened. Brook is a psychopath.'

The words became more descriptive of what had happened. 'It was just plain robbery. We got about £400 and a lot of cheques. Why he had to try and kill the other two I don't know.'

He said: 'He has got a cold, intensive look about his eyes.' He told the detectives that he did not have a gun and did not intend there to be a killing and when two prison officers came to take him away to serve his sentence he agreed instead to stay and make a statement.

He wrote it himself, telling how he broke in through a window at the back of the house, through Beverley's bedroom where he thought the panda on the bed was a person, and into the hall where the dog was lying. He unlocked the back door with some keys he found including the one for the VW he had seen outside, and let in Brook.

While they were searching for money the two women came in and Mrs Patience was hysterical, upsetting Brook because of what she said about people not being able to go into their own homes without being robbed by people like them.

Then Bob Patience arrived and said that he had not got the safe keys.

Johnson said that he thought Bob's attitude was wrong, that he was an incredibly stupid man. Then Brook shot his wife, an accident to frighten Bob. 'I was particularly disgusted that Mr Patience had allowed it to happen,' he wrote arrogantly, the cheap hoodlum out on a robbery who felt he was above the man whom he was robbing. 'As a result he promptly went with the keys to the safe and brought back the money in a blue bag which he threw at my feet.'

He told how he hoped that Mrs Patience would live, how he fetched a towel and did what he could for her, how he tied Beverley and her father up, Beverley loosely.

'It was only then that I saw John with a look I had never seen before. I had a feeling but I couldn't put it into words.'

He left ahead of Brook but as he went he heard two more shots and then Brook followed. They took the VW, drove for four or five miles before abandoning it and then walking across countryside until they came to a disused railway track.

Brook found it difficult going with only one eye and

when it began to rain heavily, even more so. Finally they took shelter in a wartime pillbox until eight in the morning, by which time Brook said that he could not remember what had happened.

They shared the money in the pillbox and burnt the cheques before hitching a lift to Chelmsford and catching a train to London to split up.

He went on writing his statement, saying that what he had said about Brook having no recollection of the shooting was a lie. He wrote, 'John is mentally ill, I know that for a fact. He said to me when we were sheltering under the tree that what he had done would ensure we would have no witnesses. Under the tree he told me he had made sure by shooting Beverley through the back to her heart and Robert through the head, quietly laughing as he told me.'

He said that the robbery was Brook's idea, probably from some information he had been given, and that he knew he had a loaded gun that night.

He went on 'I now consider that everything, the trial of Ince, was my responsibility. In fact the whole episode should never have been.'

It was what the police wanted. He had given details such as the way the house had been broken into which had been kept from the press so that only one of the real robbers could have known. It also showed that while police were looking for the robbers in the big league of East End crooks the actual culprits were the scum of the crime world, evil, nasty little men.

White and Harris went to see Brook who denied that he was with Johnson and that in fact he had lent the gun to him some time before. He could only think the Barn raid was carried out by Johnson – and George Ince.

It was a case of crooks falling out, each blaming each other.

The detectives went back to Johnson and he gave them some more information about the escape: the bank bags, a bunch of keys and a lighter were buried in the pillbox and he had thrown away a briefcase he was carrying. Police traced a workman who had found it at the spot Johnson gave.

It took longer to find the pillbox but when they did they

found the confirmation for Johnson's story and other information he gave them was checked and found to be true.

By the time the third Barn Restaurant murder trial started at Chelmsford in January 1974 Ince was starting a fifteen-year sentence, imposed three months earlier at the Old Bailey, for his part in the silver bullion robbery, a part he strongly denied. The judge told him that as he had played for high stakes so the penalty must be high too.

It was said at the trial by one of the East End defendants: 'We live in a jungle.' If that was so, the two who appeared at Chelmsford were of the lower order. They both pleaded not guilty to murder, robbery and in Brook's case attempted murder.

The jury were told that there had been two previous trials but those depended on identification and the Crown had to accept that by identifying George Ince the Patiences had been wrong. This time the proof did not depend on identification 'in any sense'. The gun owned by Brook was the one that shot the Patiences, he had boasted of doing it and Johnson had confessed although that was evidence only against him and not Brook.

Mr Oliver Martin QC, who was defending Brook, gave a hint during the first day of what the defence might be. He said the fact that the Patience family had identified Ince but that he had later been acquitted did not necessarily mean they were wrong, a point the judge, Mr Justice Stocker, agreed was right.

Bob Patience was first witness but he was not asked to try to identify either of the two men in the dock. It would be evidence, said the judge, that would be unsatisfactory.

Bob and Mr Martin then clashed time after time during the cross-examination. Bob said that he had never actually picked out Ince, saying that he was similar and that Brook was the man who had shot his wife.

Mr Martin said that the defence had information, which had been supplied by the prosecution, that Bob had been involved in the silver bullion robbery, and more, had been with Ince at a meeting where the robbery was planned and that for some reason he owed people involved in the robbery money and that he had not paid up.

Bob was livid as he denied the facts totally. 'I'd never met Ince until I saw him at the police court,' he declared and said the idea was ridiculous.

Beverley followed her father and she told the jury that she was not now maintaining that Ince was the gunman.

Slowly but surely the prosecution continued to call the evidence which they intended to present to the jury to support their claim that the two men in the dock were the two responsible for the robbery. It was a laborious job and took time. Such a case is not over in a flash of two or three quick questions, as films and television programmes suggest. It is a time-consuming matter which needs non-stop concentration by those in court whether they be judge, jury or counsel.

Little bits of information that were different came out. The petty thief who had originally tipped off the police about Brook, said that he had told him that Ince would get off because it was he (Brook) and his brother who had done it.

Detective Chief Superintendent White was asked by the defence about a suggestion that for some time there had been police suspicion that Bob Patience was a fence.

The senior detective said this was the first he had heard of it and that Mr Patience was one of his main prosecution witnesses.

The prosecution case came to an end with the last witness, Bob Patience, who was recalled. Mr Martin wanted to question him again about the bullion robbery and other matters, as he put it.

Firstly, Mr Martin asked if his swimming-pool might be used to house some of the stolen silver bullion. Bob protested that his character was being blackened and it was not on. He was told that Mr Martin was just doing his job with information with which he had been supplied.

The defence counsel then turned to the Ranch shooting and whether Bob had been kidnapped. He said that was a strong word but he agreed that as he left his home three or four men ushered him into a car and he was taken to the office of an east London engineering firm where he was told, 'it would be for my own good if I kept quiet.

'When I arrived there the manager, whom I knew

socially and was a member of the Ranch House Club, was sitting behind his desk and his words to me were that I should take heed of what was about to be said to me.

'It was explained to me that there were seventeen witnesses of the incident outside the club and that it was obvious that as manager of the club I would have all the details of their addresses etc.

'They wanted me to assure them that I would contact all these members and I should advise them it was advisable they should have bad memories.'

To emphasize the point a man he did not know although he believed he had connections with the Krays, opened a window and shot out of it. 'It only barks once,' he said and Bob took that as a comment to frighten him.

Had he met the Krays? No, he had not and did not wish to. Then, after three trials and the tension that they and the death of his wife had brought, he was allowed to go.

Mr Martin opened the defence by saying, 'This case is probably unique in criminal history. You may never know the truth of what happened on the morning of 5 November but you are not here to solve the conundrum "who killed Mrs Patience?" like a detective novel. The issue is: was Brook there?'

Brook's defence was that he was not and that he had lent his gun to Johnson that weekend and got it back by hand delivery from a man he did not know some time later. He said time after time that he had nothing to do with the murder and robbery. And two of his witnesses, the men who had picked out George Ince as being the man in the pub in Felsted, said that after seeing Brook they had not changed their minds, and they still said it was Ince.

In the bizarre sequence that followed sequence in the trial, there was even some suggestion that George Ince be called as a defence witness. That came about because one prospective defence witness, a man serving seven years for a crime involving a gun, was saying that he had met Ince in Brixton and he had confessed to being the Barn murderer. This was hearsay and the only way to test the truth was to call George Ince. The trouble there was that he might lay himself open to perjury if he changed his original story and the position was reached – with the jury out of court – that the Director of Public Prosecutions said he would not prosecute Ince for any crime if he confessed.

The judge ruled the gunman's evidence as inadmissible so he was not called and to no one's surprise, neither was George.

Johnson then went into the witness box and told how the decision to rob the Barn was taken and how Brook told him there was ten grand in the safe. There was no mention of a gun.

They went down and had a look at the Barn on Saturday 4 November, considered it an easy job and went to Chelmsford to the cinema to kill time and saw *The Italian Job*, ironically a film about a bullion robbery.

The first time he knew Brook had a gun was when the two women came into the house and Brook drew it from his raincoat pocket. Johnson said, 'I couldn't believe it. I can't remember whether I said it aloud or to myself but I said "Oh God no!" '

He repeated the story he had told the police and said that when they had got away and they were resting under a tree he asked Brook about the other two shots and he laughed as he said, 'There's no witnesses now.'

Later, when they met up again in January, Brook told him the police had got him, meaning Ince, for the part Brook had played, but not him, Johnson.

When Mr Martin began to cross-examine him, he asked if Johnson had ever heard of Walter Mitty who used to have fantasies about himself, and whether he thought of himself as such a character. No, said Johnson although psychiatrists had suggested he was. 'I know when I am telling a lie and when I am not,' he insisted.

The two men in the dock did not look at each other as both gave evidence but they had to be separated on their way down to the cells on one occasion when Brook gave vent to his fury at the betrayal he claimed his friend was making.

On 14 February, St Valentine's Day, the twenty-third day of the trial, the judge finished his summing up and the matter was left to the jury. It was for them to decide whether the two in the dock were guilty or not.

They were out just short of two and a half hours and

they found Brook guilty of the murder of Mrs Patience;
Johnson was not guilty of murder but of the alternative
charge, manslaughter. The foreman read out their
decision of guilty on the two charges of attempted murder
against Brook and found both men guilty of robbery.

The judge immediately told Mr Martin that he was not
going to make a recommendation that Brook should serve
a minimum period of the automatic life sentence which
followed the jury's verdict. Sometimes judges do this, as
happened with the Krays and others; it makes any speech
by the defending barrister pointless. Nothing Martin
could say could change the mandatory life sentence under
the law. For Johnson it was different. His counsel Mr
Patrick Back QC started to make his speech in mitigation.

It was stopped because someone chose that moment to
ring the police and tell them there was a bomb in the
courtroom. The chances of this being so were very slight
but the police had to go through the motions, so the court
was cleared and the two guilty men taken to the cells.
Brook had another go at the man who had landed him jail
for life and the prison officers had to pull them apart.

When the court resumed after no bomb had been found,
Brook was brought up on his own and sentenced and then
Mr Back made his address.

He said Johnson's behaviour was out of character, probably motivated by greed. But what had happened was that
he had allowed himself to be 'harnessed to a tiger'. He
added:

'His criminal record is petty and puerile. At the end of
the day he finds himself standing side by side with a man
convicted of one of the worst and most notorious series of
shootings that has happened since the war.'

The judge took the point and told Johnson:

'In many ways this is a sad case. I accept and it is
manifest that you are both articulate and intelligent. There
could have been no reason why you should not have led a
full and happy life. I agree the phrase that you harnessed
yourself to a tiger is probably apt.

'The gravity of your offence is very much less than that
of Brook but nonetheless I am bound to reflect the horror
that anybody must feel even at the degree of complicity

which I accept was your part in this outrage.'

He jailed him for a total of ten years. Johnson smiled as he was led into the prison van.

The twelve jurors went home under police guard because someone rang the home of one of them to say he would be harmed if Brook was convicted.

It never happened, but like most things in the Barn case, matters were not what they seemed.

What was clear was that the two men responsible for the terrible things that occurred in the lounge of Sun Lido House were behind bars and that George Henry Ince, who was also behind bars for another crime he claimed he had not committed, was a victim of mistaken identity.

It is easy to say that such things should not happen but ... how many times do people say 'Isn't that so and so?' and it turns out not to be whom they think it is? Many people do look similar to the point where mistaken identity is possible and that is in broad daylight or in a pub or restaurant or in the street where there is no stress, no fear.

How much more difficult it is for someone arriving home in the early hours to find two men, one clearly armed, waiting to rob them in poor lighting. In their terror do they note every detail that will help the police find them and then the victims identify them on a parade, mixed with eleven others who look the same?

First Muriel and Beverley, then Bob, were held by the gunman, then Muriel was shot and then Bob and Beverley. They were shot because the gunman did not want anyone left who could identify him or his accomplice. The man who was originally the suspect and the man who was finally convicted as the killer after three long trials were alike, did answer the description that Beverley and her father provided in their shaken state after the appalling thing that was done to them and a person they loved.

It is possible that they were only too anxious to identify someone, sure at the time that he was the man responsible. It only needed one juror to have thought the same and George Henry Ince would have been convicted.

Bob Patience went back to his restaurant which he sold in 1977 and retired. He died in April 1982 at the age of sixty-three.

3

Mary Kriek

A Dutch Prediction

Mary Kriek was a fair-haired nineteen-year-old girl from Voorberg, Holland, who came to England because her sister Willi was a mother's help at a farm at Eight Ash Green, a village on the A604 not far from Colchester.

In December 1957 she arrived at Bullbanks Farm and settled down at once. She was a happy, quiet girl, liked by everyone who knew her.

Before she left Holland two things happened. Mary had her horoscope read as was the national custom and she was told 'Someone will try and get rid of you', a warning of which she took no notice. The other thing she did was to buy a bright red leather diary in which she wrote the names of the families her sister gave her as contacts for her arrival in Essex.

After a few days in England she went home for Christmas, catching the ferry from Harwich, just down the road, to The Hook and then came back again. She saw her sister who worked for the Fearons, Roger and Elizabeth, at another farm in the village and became friendly with a German girl, Renate Krummeck, who worked for an American officer down the road.

The two girls went out together on their nights off and early in January, 1958, they went to London for the weekend. It was a normal weekend for girls like that in those days. They saw the sights, went to the pictures and stayed at a relative of Renate's and caught an evening train from from Liverpool Street Station to Colchester, catching one of the last buses from Colchester to Halstead at 10.30 p.m. on Sunday, 5 January 1958.

The conductor, Bertie French, knew Renate but not Mary. The two girls sat downstairs for the short ride to the hamlet and when the bus stopped at Gallows Corner for Bullbanks Farm, Mary and a woman got off. Mary waved to Renate and appeared to face the wrong way; she then turned towards the farm and was last seen walking the right way.

The only strange thing about the bus ride was that the bus overran the stop near the farm by about a hundred yards. It might momentarily have puzzled the Dutch girl as to where she was but she was certainly walking in the right direction when last seen.

It was a cold moonlit night by a fairly busy trunk road to the port of Harwich and the main route from the Midlands in those days. She had but a few yards to walk before she was home.

She did not reach the farm.

The next day tractor driver Leslie Peck found the body of a girl in a ditch as he drove to work at Boxted, fourteen miles from the bus stop. It was Mary and she had been beaten to death.

She had seventeen wicked wounds to her head and her skull had been fractured. Her hands were bruised and bones were fractured, suggesting that the killer had smashed them as she tried to defend herself from the homicidal attack in the Essex countryside.

But who would want to do it and why?

The crime started a major inquiry and received publicity for a long time both in Britain, with repercussions that are still going on, and on the Continent because she was Dutch.

Essex police were soon on the scene and Detective Superintendent Jack Barkway, head of the county CID, was in charge with Detective Inspector George Kemp, who was in charge of the Colchester division, giving him expert local back-up.

The first question they had to try to solve was whether the killer was someone who saw Mary walking just the few yards from the bus stop to the farm, pulled up, offered her a lift which was accepted and then drove off. It was something that was totally out of her character.

Or had she arranged to meet someone out of sight of the farm, gone with them – which was equally out of character – and then when the man made advances, resisted and he in his panic because she knew who he was, killed her so that he would not be given away either to his wife or girlfriend?

The inquiries spread out in two directions: to interview all of those who knew her in the short time since she arrived from Holland and to talk to anyone who might have seen her get off the bus, or seen anyone acting suspiciously in the area that night, or seen Mary with a man in the very few days preceding her death because if she had had a boyfriend she had hardly time to get to know him. Again out of character.

Her employers could not help nor could the couple who employed sister Willi. Mary's handbag had been taken when she was dumped in the ditch and in that was the little red diary in which she had written the names and addresses she had been given and might well contain an entry of the person she was due to meet that January Sunday night if, indeed, she was going to meet such a person.

It has never been found.

The police started searching the routes, country back roads, lanes, tracks, from Eight Ash Green, every way a killer could have driven to take her there. They used dogs and men.

They interviewed people by the hundreds, by the thousands, in an attempt to pick up a lead that might point them in the direction of the killer.

By the time the inquest was held in April they had interviewed 20,000 people, taken hundreds of statements, checked 5,000 vehicles and visited 4,000 houses to talk to people.

The cars were checked because a witness saw a two-tone American-style car in the area on the Sunday night with a 'Q' registration. 'Q' was the letter reserved for foreigners and not far away was the enormous American Air Force base at RAF Wethersfield where lonely men with money to burn were always on the look-out for girls. The description was vague but sufficient for detectives who were hungry for leads. They followed dozens.

There was the man who handed in bloodstained clothing at a launderette. It turned out he had cut himself while sawing.

There was the man who heard blood-curdling screams the night Mary was taken from the roadside and killed. He was ex-actor Wallace Lupino, brother of the renowned star of Lambeth Walk fame, Lupino Lane, and brother of film star Ida, who ran a pub at Ardleigh, just over three miles from the ditch in which Mary's body was found. The distance might seem far but in the still of a freezing night in a flat farming area sounds carry for miles.

He said he was woken by the screams just after one in the morning of her murder and listened to them, the blood-curdling cries of a girl in agony or scared to death. He got out of bed but could not see anything across the moonlit landscape and as the screaming stopped he went back to bed. No one can ever say whether it was Mary or not.

Then there was the car that matched the vague description they had, two-tone and American-looking, which was found in a street in Hampstead. It was an estate car and the police arrived in force. Fingerprints were taken after house-to-house inquiries revealed that it belonged to no one in the area. The prints were sent to the Criminal Record Office to see if they matched any known criminal. They did not. The number plate was checked and for a while it was thought to be a stolen vehicle. But then, after police had kept watch for several days, a man came out of one of the flats and walked up to the car. The police pounced and found that far from being a killer the man was a musician who was cheating on his wife by having a few nights of illicit love with his girlfriend. The car belonged to a friend who was out of the country and the reason why he had not gone to it for several days was because he was having such a good time with his girl.

All these events and inquiries, involving at least 200 policemen, were going on in a wide area, spreading through Colchester and within ten-mile radii of the spot where she got off the bus and where her body was found.

At the same time Superintendent Barkway and his top

detectives were homing in on the major characters closely involved in the murder, her parents, her sister, her friend, employers and their friends.

Willi, two years older than Mary, and working in the area for a year, told police the names of all the people to whom she wrote letters of introduction when Mary arrived. She told them everything she knew about Mary and her life from their childhood up to the day she died and it was a simple story of a girl from a good happy home who was perfectly normal without deep secrets or any skeletons in the cupboard.

The detectives spoke to Renate. She told them how she met Mary at a Christmas party at Colchester Technical College, how they went to the pictures together because they had no boyfriends, how they had gone to London and seen Buckingham Palace and the Tower of London and had caught the train and then the No. 88 bus home. They talked on the bus and planned to meet very soon. Because they talked and talked Mary missed her normal stop which was when the conductor noticed too and stopped the bus. Renate saw Mary walking on her own towards the farm.

She said: 'She had no boyfriends in England and had in fact only been out of the farm five times. I was her best friend in England and I know that she was a very nice, quiet and religious girl.'

Mary's employer endorsed this but added a strange conversation she had with Mary just before she left for her trip to London (which included seeing a film called *Count Five and Die*). She had said: 'If I don't come back you'll get a little black card.' Mary did not come back but no one got a little black card.

They talked to Roger St Clair Fearon, Willi's employer, who was also not able to help. But it was he who went to meet the girls' father Anton at Harwich when he landed from Holland. The police kept the press, reporters and photographers away from the quayside so they took photographs as the cars sped by and some press vehicles gave chase.

What he saw angered Mr Fearon so much that he started making a list of what he regarded as press intrusion and wrote to *The Times*. His bitter attack caused a row which many prominent people joined. More of that shortly, because Mr Fearon's part in the inquiry went on too.

Mr Kriek had no complaint. The police showed him where Mary was last seen and where she was found; they told him how his daughter had died with seventeen crushing blows on the back and top of her skull with a metal or iron bar and how she tried to protect herself.

Mr Kriek sat with Willi, twenty-one and bespectacled, in the Fearons' home at Earls Colne, just down the road from Eight Ash Green, and discussed every possible person who could have met her and treated her in this way. They could think of no one.

He told the police about her red diary, how she had a list of contacts in it, how he would get a similar one and a similar leather handbag when he went back to Holland.

The next day he went to the opening of the inquest and afterwards said:

'I have no bitterness for England because I have lost my daughter here. I have no bitterness towards the murderer. Mary will be buried here tomorrow,' and then he thanked the press for their kindness.

Mary was buried in Colchester cemetery and for the first time in a murder case, a photographer was allowed at the funeral so that the pictures he took could be taken back to Holland for her distraught mother.

As police went on with their search for the killer whom they described as a maniac who could have taken one of twenty-seven routes to the ditch where Mary was found, Mr Fearon started writing.

In his letter to *The Times* in January 1958 he said under the headline: 'Reporting a murder: how the press behaved':

A week ago a friend of mine was murdered near here.

May I now place on record the conduct of the majority of the national papers in connection with this affair?

Within five minutes of the murdered girl's family in Holland being told of her death reporters from well-known British papers had swarmed into their flat, even penetrating to the girl's bedroom before being thrown out. No other reporters from any other country including Holland itself took part in this disgraceful scramble.

It is significant that the newspaper which was in the lead in Holland was also the first in the field here – perhaps they are proud of this?

Here we, who knew the family best, were subjected to a ceaseless stream of journalists all wanting scraps of gossip. This we declined to do – only the police could and did give them facts but this apparently does not satisfy them. One reporter even threatened to make up some news if I did not give him any and this he did two days later.

The next degrading step in the hunt for news came when I met the murdered girl's father and sister at Harwich. Their landing in this country was obviously a most painful moment for them, yet as soon as we drove out of the dock gates there was a scramble to take photos of the unfortunate pair and a queue of about five cars containing photographers followed me closely to my home. I stopped once and asked them to have some regard for the relatives' feelings but this only acted as a spur for they proceeded to pass, one by one, taking flashlight photos as they passed. The effect on the couple with me was ghastly and I could only feel bitterly ashamed and apologise for the Press' behaviour.

Later on there was even a cameraman who wanted to photograph these two as they went to see the girl's body – surely one of the most distressing moments it is possible to imagine.

During this past week I have spoken to many people in many walks of life and every single one has condemned this ghastly behaviour. I mention this as one always hears that 'the public only gets the news it wants' and yet this does not appear to be so. Can nothing be done to stop this disgusting kind of thing? Is this the sort of thing the Press Council is interested in?

Now I would like to turn to the other side of the picture and mention the authorities with whom both I and the relatives have come into contact – the Essex police and the Immigration and Customs authorities at Harwich. From the very first all of those have shown sympathy and consideration which I have never seen equalled. Through the courtesy of the Chief Immigration and Preventive Officers at Harwich the relatives were able to land and later depart without delay or any distressing formalities. The kindness, courtesy and sympathy of the Essex police officers in all their dealings with the relatives have been beyond praise and have made the deepest possible impression upon them.

What a contrast there is between this impression of the British police and that of the British press which they have now taken back to Holland with them.

It was the kind of case the Press Council was interested in and the next day the chairman, Sir Linton Andrews, had a letter published in *The Times* saying there would be an inquiry but that some difficulties did arise when so many reporters wanted to ask questions and when so many photographers wanted to take pictures.

But what Mr Fearon had done was to stir up a hornets' nest of some considerable proportions. His letter brought many into the correspondence columns of *The Times* from people who, in many cases, knew nothing of the facts and it also brought motions of condemnation from women's organizations and church councils.

Lady Violet Bonham-Carter was the most hard-hitting in the letters column. She said:

Few can have read Mr Fearon's letter last Friday without deep shame and indignation; shame that reporters of the British press should have been guilty of the actions he describes; indignation that these outrages on common human decency should be allowed by those who have the power to prevent them. They bring disgrace not only on the good name of our press but of our country.

We read that in Holland the reporters of the British Press alone 'swarmed' into the house of the murdered girl and even penetrated to her bedroom and that from the moment her stricken family landed on British soil they were pursued by car-loads of photographers, armed with flashlights, who remained undeterred by the appeals to spare the feelings of their victims.

This pattern of behaviour is painfully familiar to us here but all the more degrading. And we must ask ourselves why it is possible for policemen, Customs officials, Immigration Officers and countless others to discharge their duties and retain intact their human instincts of sympathy and sensibility while Press reporters can and do divest themselves of every vestige of compassion and humanity.

What can we do? The law provides no remedy. Sir Linton Andrews writes truly in his letter to-day that 'no resolution of the Press Council can, by itself, be expected to produce reform'. Public opinion goes unheeded. But a few powerful men, who own and who control these newspapers and who employ others to perform these odious functions, could put a stop to them tomorrow by ordering that they should cease forthwith. Why do these men not act?

Strong stuff, and there were other letters in like vein. They were a typical reaction then – and it is the same now, for the same arguments go on – of those who did not like the press. The facts had not yet been proved, no papers actually named, but what Mr Fearon had written was taken as the truth and it brought a flood of support before the evidence had been investigated. It was always thus.

Representatives of journalism wrote saying that such behaviour was distasteful to them too and the then editor of the *Daily Mirror*, Jack Nener, took up the whole of his front page to tell his 5 million paying readers (multiply by four to find the total readership which was about half the population then) that *Mirror* staff never behaved like this. Under the enormous headline 'PRIVATE LIVES' he wrote:

An important discussion has been taking place in the correspondence columns of *The Times* over the past twelve days and also on television. It has been alleged that the parents of a murdered Dutch girl, Mary Kriek, were hounded and harassed by newspaper photographers and the Press showed no regard for their distress. The question being discussed is: does the press, on occasions, intrude into private grief?

The *Daily Mirror* has conducted a thorough inquiry into the work of its staff in reporting this tragedy. The Editor is satisfied that none of the allegations made applies to any photographer or journalist on this newspaper. This does not cause any surprise in this office.

The *Daily Mirror* has always tried to observe the accepted standards of decent behaviour and to treat all citizens with consideration and respect.

We do not claim haloes for ourselves. This is a vigorous, outspoken newspaper. We will not hesitate to expose the buffooneries of public personalities when it is in the public interest to do so. Nor, through fear of criticism or accusations of bad taste, will we flatter fools in high places or shield wrongdoers.

But we believe in the dignity of human beings. We believe that news obtained at the cost of personal distress is not worth printing.

The *Daily Mirror* pledges that its staff will always act as responsible men and women in their pursuit of news.

If at any time a reader of this or any other newspaper feels that the Mirror has broken its pledge, he or she is invited to send the complaint to: J.S. Nener, the Editor.

Strong, pungent and to the point. As a reporter on the paper at that time I and a colleague were the first to go to Bullbanks Farm and speak to the wife of Mary's employer. He had gone to London for the day with the children to a pantomime, having no idea when he left that she had been found dead or even was missing. We spoke to the wife who was not able to tell us much and referred us to the police. There was never any unpleasantness, never any trouble and during the weeks that followed – apart from the complaint about the car chase from Harwich – there was nothing to complain about. No one made up interviews, no one harassed Mr Kriek nor broke into his house, and when he left to go back to Holland he thanked the press for their courtesy.

While the Press Council investigated Mr Fearon's

complaints, the inquiry went on.

For a time it was linked to the murder of Ann Noblett, a seventeen-year-old who also vanished after getting off a bus a matter of 300 yards from her home but at Wheathampstead, Hertfordshire. Unlike Mary, Ann's body was not immediately found and when it was, four weeks later, it was not as far from her home. She was fully clothed, lying on her back in dense overgrowth in a wood at Whitwell, Herts, with some copper coins scattered around the frosty ground.

The incredible thing was that she still wore her glasses. Her body was very well preserved suggesting that it had been kept in a refrigerator of some kind from the moment she was killed. One reporter wrote that a frozen tear drop was found in one eye but far-fetched as that sounded, there was no doubt that she had been kept in a freezer.

The two police forces compared notes and although there were basic similarities – getting off buses in the dark, almost certainly accepting lifts, suggesting that they knew their killers – there was little else in common. Ann was a local girl, Mary a foreigner. Ann had been strangled and Mary beaten to death. Neither had been interfered with but Mary's killer had unceremoniously dumped her at once while Ann's had kept her hidden, probably only getting rid of the body because of fear that someone might discover it, suggesting that he lived on his own or that his wife was away.

A short time later two men were taken to Southend police station for questioning all day by detectives from Essex and Hertfordshire with the top Scotland Yard officers they had called in to run their inquiry. Essex steadfastly refused to call in the Yard like other county police forces. The press waited in the police bar as the snow fell outside and after fourteen hours one of the senior officers came in to tell them that the two men had been released having given a satisfactory explanation of their movements and that there would be no charges.

It was the end of any attempt to link the two murders. Ann Noblett's killer has never been found. No one knows where her body was kept and there has never been any sensible explanation for her murder.

There was another strange sidetracking in the Mary Kriek murder. Press and police used a pub as their headquarters slightly away from Eight Ash Green and Earls Colne. The landlord, a big bluff man, welcomed them and supplied them well with drink and fat chicken sandwiches. He kept chickens which ran about in the garden at the rear of the pub.

The only trouble as far as his neighbour, a timid former civil servant who had had to retire early, was concerned was the fact that the chickens used to come across into his garden. He complained to the landlord on a number of occasions but he did not take too much notice apart from strengthening the fence. Still the chickens crossed over and one Saturday afternoon, while the press had returned to London for Saturday which was all they had of a weekend in those days, the neighbour went to remonstrate. The landlord was busy and was in no mood to argue and told the neighbour so.

To the landlord's astonishment – and everyone else's later – the neighbour produced a gun and shot the landlord dead through the heart. The neighbour eventually arrived at Essex Assize court at Chelmsford.

The hunt for Mary's killer went on. More and more people were questioned, statements were taken, answers cross-checked. The hunt for the weapon continued and ponds were searched by frogmen. Nothing that could help in any way was discovered. A man seen in the area was traced and discounted. Americans were questioned without result.

And the Press Council duly reported their findings. They had interviewed Mr Fearon, police, the Chief Constable of Essex, reporters and photographers and their general purposes committee produced a report which said categorically at the start: 'As a result of their inquiries the Press Council have come to the conclusion that while Mr Fearon made his complaints in good faith he nevertheless made several misleading statements.'

No reporters had penetrated Mary's bedroom, no British reporters swarmed into the Krieks' house in Holland. The only reporters there were Dutch and about six of them were admitted in the usual way by Mr Kriek who later became angry and asked them to leave, which they did. There was no evidence that those who called were callous, offensive or unscrupulous.

No reporter invented information because Mr Fearon would not supply him with any. One reporter made a serious mistake by saying that a detective had been to Fearon's house to question the Krieks when in fact he only saw Fearon.

It was true that the photographers had followed the Krieks in Fearon's car from Harwich after being put in one spot by the police and had taken pictures as they went by.

The allegation that a photographer wanted to take pictures at the mortuary could not be substantiated because the Press Council could not find the photographer but their report said: 'From several sources however has come the statement that Mr and Miss Kriek willingly posed for pictures at the inquest. Afterwards through a Dutch-speaking photographer Mr Kriek told the press representatives that he had been touched by the sympathy that he had received and that he held no bitterness.'

The Press Council found that a photographer did take pictures of Fearon and the Krieks when they arrived at his house but when told he was trespassing left immediately.

Their statement ended: 'The Press Council find: that while Mr Fearon has failed to substantiate his charges made against "the majority of the national daily newspapers" there was one case of serious inaccuracy in a report, there were also two episodes of badgering intrusion i.e. the press cars' pursuit of the family on the road from Harwich and the press photographers' entry into the garden of Mr Fearon's home. These matters are strongly condemned.'

Mr Fearon said no more on the subject.

A short time later a unique conference was held at Scotland Yard when all those involved in the inquiry met to discuss every detail they knew. Detective Chief Superintendent Jack Barkway and his team were there. The pathologist Dr Jack Nicholas was there. Forensic scientists were there. About the only person who was not there was the Dutch astrologer who told Mary, 'Someone will try to put you aside and even to get rid of you' shortly before she set off for England. The girl born on 31 May under the sign of Gemini believed him, and her father said that many people in Holland believed in astrology and horoscopes but he did not know that Mary did. The astrologer later wrote to Dutch police to tell them the man who killed Mary was aged forty and born on a date in August, a fact they passed over to the Essex police.

But like the conference it led to nothing and Mary's killer was still at large, just as he is today.

The full inquest was finally held and after Detective Chief Superintendent Barkway had told how many thousands had been interviewed, how police using dogs and mine detectors had searched every road and by-way round Bullbanks Farm, a verdict of murder by person or persons unknown was recorded.

There was a strange footnote.

Some time after the murder Roger St Clair Fearon, the moustached, tall Cambridge graduate farmer and former special constable who so hated the press and their activities, left his English wife for their latest Dutch au pair, Fritia.

They married in England in late 1959 after he had divorced his wife and they went to Australia to start a new life in Melbourne.

One day in May 1961, three years after Mary's murder, police received a mysterious phone call from the former special constable saying there was something wrong at his home.

When asked what it was he said 'Death'.

The police raced to the house to find two bodies, that of Fearon and his Dutch wife, aged thirty, who was in his arms. He had shot her before killing himself.

He was forty-three.

A note said: 'We desire to be together always, even in death. Please cremate us and preserve our ashes together.'

His former wife said curtly, 'His wife used to work for us as a servant.'

An Essex police official statement said: 'He was never a suspect. He was interviewed like many others but only because he employed Mary's sister.'

4

Hanson

An Evil Pair

Colchester is Britain's oldest town. It has always been a
military town and in 1978 newly-weds Private Michael
Hanson and his fair-haired wife Carol moved into a
married quarter on the large Montgomery estate at the
barracks.

Within a few weeks of their marriage Michael, who like
his wife was twenty-four, was posted to Kenya for six
weeks. While he was away she began to play, not with
other men as often happens but with the children who
came to her semi in Fallowfield Road. In the little
two-bedroomed house Carol, who had shoulder-length
hair and a pasty complexion which matched her
heaviness, behaved in a way that soon became something
that was whispered about but not really believed.

Carol insisted they came to see her dog, a pointer called
Sally. But later girls told how they went to the house and
sometimes Carol would take one upstairs to the bedroom
and there they would undress each other and sex acts
would take place.

Other children took part in the striptease games and
they went on until Michael of the Royal Anglian
Regiment came back from his training exercise.

He joined in.

On 16 March another soldier's daughter, Christine
Jones (not her real name) who was ten, went swimming at
the Garrison Pool and never came home. She was seen
going to the Hansons' home but no one to this day knows
why she did. It may have been out of curiosity, it may
have been by invitation, but no one has ever explained it.

But later that night her body was found under some bushes in Eight Ash Road not far from the estate. She had been stabbed twice in the chest, partially strangled and sexually assaulted.

The police started making inquiries and neighbours of the newly-weds told how they heard a young child screaming and then shortly afterwards Hanson, a burly, surly man, had been seen leaving the house carrying what appeared to be a white sack.

The next day after the body had been found he joked to a neighbour that he had murdered the little girl. The police heard of that and when Hanson was taken in for questioning by the police he told many varied and misleading stories, changing them to say one thing, altering it to another.

Police searched the house and found the knife. Neighbours handed them some strange pornographic pictures that were part of the newly-weds' private collection.

They were charged and in July came up for trial at Hertford in front of Mr Justice Melford Stevenson, a judge with a hard reputation. He stood no nonsense as the Kray twins, for example, discovered when they appeared in front of him. After they had been convicted of murder he told them, 'I think it is time that the public had a rest from your activities,' and sentenced them to a minimum of thirty years with their life sentences.

He also sentenced the Cambridge rapist, a cunning thief who turned to rape almost by accident when robbing a bedsit, his speciality, in the university which is full of such apartments. The girl was just getting out of the bath and Peter Samuel Cook, who had been to prison several times for his dishonesty, took the opportunity. He revelled in his notoriety as he prowled bedsit land which he knew better than any policeman hunting him, and as his fame grew so did his daring. He made a mask with zip slits for the eyes and mouth and the word 'Rapist' painted in white across the top. It matched the personality of the little man who had talked his way into Broadmoor for one robbery. They soon found he was sane. Eventually he was caught and appeared at Norwich where he admitted a string of rapes.

Melford Stevenson, who did not like them, observed that Cook had acquired a certain skill in talking to psychiatrists and sent him to prison for life saying that however it might upset do-gooders, in his case life should really mean life.

So there were the soldier and his plump wife in the dock in front of a man who had heard it all before. He had tried George Ince in the first Barn trial and then while the retrial was going on heard a shocking story of an escaped burglar who found lodgings with an unhappily married couple, fell in love with the wife who reciprocated and he killed the husband (see Chapter 2.) This was a judge it was difficult to shock but the Hansons succeeded. Mr Basil Wigoder, QC, prosecuting, told the jury that after the screams Hanson was seen to carry a white sack from the house in which was the little girl's body.

The Hansons went to the police and Michael Hanson told them that on the night Christine died he had been walking with his dog and found her towel on the ground.

From then on, Mr Wigoder said, the soldier made numerous misleading statements. He said he had never seen the girl before but then said that she had called at the house, he had let her in and left her with his wife downstairs. He then had a row with his wife and left the house and when he returned he found the girl dead on the bed.

He told the police in that particular statement as he started blaming his wife – and she in return blamed him, which went on throughout the trial:

'It was terrible and made me sick,' so he said he wrapped her in a cloth, put her under the bushes and then went back to clean the knife. It was a flick knife and police found it in a roll of lavatory paper in the bathroom.

Mrs Hanson however said that she had never seen the girl and had hidden the flick knife because she thought it was illegal to possess one. It was.

Hanson added another story line during those first interviews. He said that his wife suffered from epilepsy and got all worked up. He had gone to the pub and when he returned he found his wife lying on the bed with the girl, the flick knife on the dressing-table.

'I had to slap my wife's face a couple of times to bring her round. I carried the body downstairs. I told my wife I would not tell anyone.'

The next day the jury heard more from the statements that the couple made to the police. Carol told them that twice he had tried to strangle her and when they told her what he had said in his statement blaming her she declared:

'Lies all lies. I didn't think he hated me that much. What is he trying to do to me? I didn't even know the girl.'

Then she said the girl had never been in the house and when her husband came back from the pub with some pop after being away for only a few minutes he told her that a girl had been murdered. She did not believe him so he said he would show her. He did and she ended the statement, 'I didn't even know the girl. I expect he did it.'

The matron in the cells at Colchester police station told how she had a conversation with Carol who said: 'I didn't do it, my husband did.'

At the same time her husband was telling a prisoner he met in the cells: 'I'm inside for killing a little girl but it wasn't me, it was my wife. She killed her in a fit.'

So the scene was set for the bizarre trial that followed with each blaming the other. They had both denied the murder and doing the little girl grievous bodily harm and Private Hanson was charged with sexually assaulting Christine too.

Just what went on as a matter of course in the house was described by a girl of fifteen who was a regular caller. She said they played a stripping game called 'love, true, dare – double dare – kiss and promise' and the point of it was to take off your clothes and end up almost naked. The regular winner who got down to her pants while her husband was away, was Carol Hanson, the girl said. Boys and girls, aged between eleven and fifteen played the game.

Another girl said she had never been touched but the next witness was a doctor who had examined all the children who had gone to the house for the games and found evidence of sexual assault in every case.

The girl aged fourteen, who wept as she gave evidence

said: 'Several times I was taken into the bedroom by Mrs Hanson. She used to undress me and I would undress her. We would get on the bed together and she would play with my breasts.'

Carol would also play with her with the handle of a knife.

The man who shared the cell with Private Hanson in Colchester police station added more fuel against Mrs Hanson, for he related what Hanson told him. 'He said the little girl had been to the house before. He said his wife used to interfere with her sexually and that his wife was over-sexed.'

He had said that he and his wife had rows and 'she has a terrible temper and throws things about. Once I had to punch her. The worst is when she has fits. She goes really bad. They are terrible. If she does not have her tablets there is no knowing what will happen. If she is upset she has the fits.'

And then the soldier went into the witness box himself to fix his wife.

She had three illegitimate children and while he was on the training exercise in Kenya she wrote to him and said that not only had the children been at the house but she had been unfaithful to him.

On 16 March the little girl came to the house. The burly soldier said, as his wife sat staring at him from the dock:

'The girl said she knew something that my wife had done to some of her friends. My wife got in a temper and lost control. She jumped for the girl and shook her round the neck. I managed to pull her off and I told the girl to go but she couldn't seem to stand on her feet. I held her up by the arm. She was choked I suppose.

'Then my wife grabbed the girl from behind. I couldn't see what was done until it was all over. The girl had been stabbed. I didn't know my wife had a knife until I took it off her.'

Later he took the little girl's body out and dumped it.

The woman who told police that her husband was a funny chap who clouted her when she did not do as she was told but things were all right by the time they got to bed, did not move a muscle. Then as the court ended for the day she went down the steps to the cells below the court without any acknowledgement of her husband.

Her husband who denied ever sexually assaulting the little girl even though the medical evidence showed there had been an attempt to have intercourse, followed her down expressionless.

The next day Mr Basil Wigoder QC cross-examined him. The barrister asked:

'Christine was killed by you and your wife as part of some kind of perverted pleasure?'

Not so, said Hanson. 'The only part I played was in taking the body outside.'

'This child was stabbed at the same time as she was being sexually assaulted by you. She was killed by you and your wife as part of some form of perverted sexual pleasure?'

No, no, said Hanson. 'No, that child was not sexually assaulted. I never strangled her. I never stabbed her and I never sexually assaulted her.'

Then he was asked by his wife's counsel: 'I suggest not only that you wickedly committed this crime but that you are now wickedly trying to blame your wife.'

Hanson replied smartly, 'That is not true. I have told the truth.'

If it was the truth his wife was guilty. But she maintained that it was her husband who was the wicked murderer.

Her counsel, Mr Barry Hudson QC went for Hanson head on.

'You murdered that child didn't you?' he demanded.

'No,' Hanson whispered.

'And murdered her on your own?'

'No I didn't.'

'So your wife murdered this child while you went to the public house?'

Hanson said, 'That's right.'

'You bear no responsibility for this girl's death at all?'

'No.' He was emphatic.

But what about the fifty letters Hanson wrote to his wife while they were on remand in different prisons? In one he said, 'My darling Carol, I'm sorry I told a big lie but I'm getting it worked out now. You have nothing to worry about. You can rely on me, my love.'

Hanson told the barrister, 'I told my wife not to worry and I would take the blame.'

'If this is true your wife committed a desperately evil thing in your presence.'

Hanson held his head high as he said, 'I have told the truth.'

He was asked about his behaviour with his wife in front of the children.

'We were only kissing,' he said, and the children only came round while he was in Kenya.

Then it was his wife's turn. Brushing back her shoulder-length hair she gave her opinion of her husband's evidence: 'He is lying, I am brighter than he is.'

If anyone was expecting an answer as to what had gone on in the past in that House of Horrors in general and what went on the night when little Christine – if the husband was anywhere near right – had threatened to tell, they were disappointed. Mrs Hanson said she just did not know, had never seen the girl, did not know anything about anything. 'To the best of my ability I have told the police the truth,' she insisted.

The prosecution had alleged that Christine had been to the house to take part in the depraved games. What games, the wife asked. There were no games.

'Many boys and girls used to come to our house to see me,' she admitted freely. 'But they never played any sex games. They used to like to take the dog out.'

The judge stepped in. 'Are you telling the jury that each of these little girls had no more interest in you than the dog?'

'Yes, as far as I know. There was no other reason to my knowledge,' she insisted.

Her explanation for the night of the murder was simple. She had spent the day cleaning the house and the brasses as she listened to records. She was a little deaf but she did hear furniture being moved about upstairs where her husband was cleaning his kit. Her dog did not bark to indicate anything was wrong.

Later he came down and said he had put a bed cover in the boiler and after he came back from the pub he told her that a little girl had been murdered round the corner.

She told the jury: 'I didn't believe him because he was always making jokes in this particular fashion. On the previous Saturday he said he had been in some woods and strangled a girl.'

Then the Joker, she said, invited her to go with him. 'Come on,' he said, 'I'll show you.' She went on: 'I went with him to a cul-de-sac and saw something that looked like a piece of material or paper.'

Mr Wigoder cross-examined her but she would not budge.

'Didn't Christine come round to your house as other little girls had come round so that there might be these various sexual acts by you with them?'

'No that's untrue. I had never seen Christine.'

She did admit that she had told a girl of fifteen who used to come to the house – the noise of the visits was so great that neighbours sometimes complained – that if she ever caught her husband with another woman she would go for him.

Mr Wigoder asked: 'Did you not say you would go for the woman? We have heard that your husband had intercourse with Christine. Didn't you go for the woman with one of the knives that intrigue you so much?'

'No, I didn't see her so how could I go for her?' There was no doubt in her voice at all. She emphasized the point.

'I never heard her being assaulted, strangled or stabbed. I never heard her screaming. I never heard my husband clearing up the mess and I never heard him leaving the house with the body.'

'If your account of that night is true then your husband must have killed the girl?'

Mrs Hanson gave a flick of her hair. 'It seems that way to me. He lied when he gave evidence.'

The case was adjourned overnight. The well-matched couple did not look at each other and went down to the cells; the legal and journalist men and women and the public went out gladly into the fresh air.

The start next day was held up. Instead of getting to his feet to cross-examine Mrs Hanson on behalf of her husband – and the jury were clearly expecting some very sharp questions indeed – Mr Leslie Boreham QC, now a Lord Justice, went down to the cells to have a conversation with his client at Hanson's urgent request. Such conversations carry the confidentiality of a doctor and his patient, of the priest and the penitent in the confessional box.

After two hours while everyone else connected with the case drank tea in the canteen room upstairs or waited outside on the steps of the court, Mr Boreham and his instructing solicitor and his junior, for a QC always had to have a junior to help him as a matter of course, reappeared from below ground. In came the jury and up from the cells came the husband and wife.

Mr Boreham dropped a bombshell in his soft gentle voice that had held juries spellbound over the years.

'I have no questions to ask this witness,' he said and sat down. He also said shortly afterwards that he did not propose to address the jury with a closing speech that normally would have underlined that his client was not guilty of the charges and the reasons for saying so.

Instead Mr Wigoder made a speech for the prosecution, underlining the way that both had blamed the other and how the evidence against both of them fitted.

Mr Hudson then told the jury that Mrs Hanson had told them that she was not responsible and that her husband had committed the terrible murder. He made all the points he could to sustain her defence.

The jury were out for a little over three hours and came back to return a verdict of guilty of murder against both the Hansons and found the soldier guilty of unlawful sexual intercourse with the girl.

The judge did not waste words. He said there was no point in making any observation about the evidence and went on:

'My only duty is to impose on each of you a sentence of imprisonment for life. In the case of each of you my recommendation is that you be detained for twenty years.'

It was the longest recommendation for a woman ever imposed in Britain. It made the *Guinness Book of Records*. Mrs Hanson did not blanch. Her pasty face remained as pasty as ever it had done.

Hanson was also sentenced to ten years for having sex with the terrified little girl in an act of degradation and wickedness worthy of the Moors murder.

What made them do it? Carol undoubtedly was oversexed. She had the first of three illegitimate children at the age of fifteen and was known as one of the wildest of the young swingers as she grew up in a Kent seaside town.

She had a fascination for knives. The flick knife her husband brought back from Africa was not only her favourite but a sexual plaything.

She could use knives too. She pulled a knife on a former lover with whom she lived for three years when he threatened to leave her. With another she attempted suicide after threatening him with a knife.

There was another lover too. When he said he was calling off the engagement she brought out a knife.

Her husband was a different sort, solid, slow, one of twelve children who had been brought up in an orphanage in the Midlands and there was nothing in his history to suggest that he would ever behave in such an awful way.

The dead girl's parents sat through the case. They could not keep away and wanted to see what kind of person could do such things to their daughter. Her father said as the Hansons were taken away:

'People talk about wrongness of capital punishment but any parents would know what I could do right now if I got the chance.'

As far as the public was concerned that was the end of it. The Hansons would be in their mid-forties when they were finally let out of jail. They would have a hard time, particularly the woman, because other prisoners do not like child-killers and have their own way of dealing with them. It may not happen at once but when a prisoner is inside for twenty years everyone has time to wait and make the apprehension even more terrible for the victim.

But there was a tailpiece to the verdict and sentence. It was this:

Why did Trooper Hanson call for his barrister and what did he say to him down in the cells, an instruction so clear that it made Mr Boreham decide not to ask any questions to try to get at the truth of what had happened in that little house nor to address the jury to try to make them see his client was not guilty? The instructions that Hanson initially gave to his solicitor who passed them on to Mr Boreham as he briefed him on the defence were that he was innocent and that his oversexed wife was completely to blame.

In March the next year, almost a year after Christine was murdered, the story behind the change of mind came out in the High Court when Carol Hanson appealed against her conviction.

Mr Barry Hudson QC told the three appeal court judges, Lord Parker of Waddington, the then Lord Chief Justice, Lord Justice Widgery and Mr Justice Cooke that after giving his evidence in which he accused his wife of the murder, Hanson called his barrister, Mr Boreham, down to the cells.

There he came out with an astonishing story. He privately admitted that he alone was responsible for the murder and that his wife had nothing to do with it.

It put the barrister very much on the spot. He could not tell the jury because of the confidential link which must be preserved under the rules of the Bar between client and lawyer. It meant that Mr Boreham could not tell the court what Hanson had told him without breaking that confidentiality. But equally, Mr Boreham could not go on defending his client as if he was innocent, which up to then he had maintained, when he knew Hanson was guilty by his own admission.

To complicate matters everyone knew that Hanson kept changing his story, dodging from guilty in letters to his wife to not guilty and blaming her in court. He made several contradictory statements to the police when first interviewed which were different from the story he told the man with whom he shared a cell.

Mr Boreham had only two courses available to him: to stay silent, not cross-examine Mrs Hanson and then make no address to the jury so that he did not break the rules of his profession, or to get Hanson to change his plea. But despite his admission he refused to do so. It left Mr Boreham in the position that he had to tell the judge and jury there would be no cross-examination which of course was really vital if Hanson's evidence that his wife killed Christine because she threatened to expose her for the sex games she played with the other children, was to be believed.

The trial ended and the terrible couple were sentenced.

It was only later in his prison cell that Hanson decided that he would waive the special confidential relationship between client and his legal team and made a statement to his solicitor.

In it Hanson said that he put all the blame on his wife because she had admitted going with another soldier while he was on army exercises in Kenya and he wanted her locked up. He said:

'I wanted to make sure my wife would be put away for the same length of time so that she would not have the opportunity to be unfaithful to me again.'

It was because of this statement that Mrs Hanson now appealed against her sentence on the grounds that if the jury had heard what her husband had told his barrister they might have taken a different view of her version; that she had nothing to do with the murder and that she never even saw nor knew the child. She asked that a new trial be ordered so that the jury would hear the fresh evidence.

As the appeal went on in the absence of the Hansons, the Lord Chief Justice said that the trial judge, Melford Stevenson, had rung him to ask for advice should there be a change of plea to guilty. Barristers often appraise judges of what is going on in a manner that is not quite direct but wrapped up in legal language which gives everyone involved an indication of what is going on. The Lord Chief Justice said in court:

'I gave him such advice as I could and then retired from the picture.'

He was now back in it as Mr Basil Wigoder QC, who had prosecuted in the trial, opposed the application. His view was that Hanson had made several conflicting statements and these had been put before the jury.

During the trial neither of them had denied that the little girl had been stabbed in their small house and neighbours, one as far as fifty yards away, had heard the child scream. It was therefore not surprising, he suggested, that the jury did not believe Mrs Hanson's story that she knew nothing of the killing. There was also the absolute fact that Christine's body was found not far from the house.

The next morning Lord Justice Widgery gave the judgement. He said that the soldier's two statements were a strange account like other versions he had given of what had happened.

The jury did not hear what was said between Hanson and his legal team and now Mrs Hanson was saying that considerable injustice had been done to her at her trial because she was not given the opportunity to answer the prejudicial allegations against her. Instead of allowing the trial to go on the judge should have stopped it and ordered a separate trial, but he did not do so.

Now Hanson's fresh evidence amounted to a confession of guilt and constituted fresh evidence to support a retrial.

But the appeal judge said if Hanson had been consistent and less eccentric and changed his plea to guilty a new trial could have been ordered.

It left Mr Justice Melford Stevenson in a considerable difficulty and no application for a new trial was made in court.

There would not be one now he said. No one could possibly credit anything Hanson said because of the way he kept changing his story. He had used truth and lie with total indifference and there was no possibility of the court ordering a retrial.

The couple stayed in prison.

Just who was responsible, what did happen and why it happened, only the Hansons knew. What piece of chemistry first attracted them only they know. It was a disastrous attachment, she the oversexed woman, he the surly burly soldier who had not had a happy life.

Whatever else he found he discovered early on that she was not going to be a faithful wife to him and that her sex drive included games with children that would shock anyone. Whether she dragged him into those games when he came back from Africa, whether he just watched, whether they were both involved in that final unbelievable game that resulted in Christine dying because she might tell, remain secrets that will haunt them for the rest of their lives.

Or perhaps not.

5

Linda Smith

The Mystery of the Red Flecks

Earls Colne lies on the A604 on the top side of the Triangle. It is not a big place but steeped in history. For many years it was a village through which the heavy lorries and cars carrying holiday-makers and servicemen passed on their way to Colchester or on to Harwich and its ferry port. The new trunk road network has changed that. The dual carriageways that link the Midlands and London and the west with the ports of the east coast and the giant container lorries, the cars, the exports, the imports they carry, sweep past Earls Colne without even knowing of its existence.

But on the evening of Monday, 16 January 1961, the lorries rumbled through in the dank, cold dark. They were as familiar a sight to the villagers as the aircraft in and out of Heathrow are to the people of Chiswick and Richmond. They are there but no one really notices them any more.

Linda Smith was twelve, a normal little girl, with darkish hair, perhaps young for her age, trusting, kind, ever willing so that she was known by some as Little Miss Friendly. She was the eldest of six children and lived just off the High Street with her parents, Robert and Pat. Linda was conscious of the fact that she was growing up and had decided to do something about it by having her pigtails cut off, leaving an urchin-style cut. It made her look her age.

At 4.50 p.m. her grandmother gave her a ten-shilling note and asked her to go to the newsagent on the High Street, just 200 yards away, to buy an evening paper for her father. Linda put on her brown coat, pulled up the hood and went out into the night.

It was cold and she hurried. Not to the newsagent, however, but first to the shop of the village cobbler who used to give her his tobacco tins when he had finished using them. Linda collected them. But this night he did not have any and she thanked him and went. A few minutes later a schoolfriend Margaret Martin, also twelve years old, saw Linda looking into the newsagent's window but she did not speak and when Margaret came out Linda had gone. That was 5.10 p.m.

She did not go home – ever.

A little later that evening a café proprietor at Great Leighs, fifteen miles away, noticed a man with a little girl in a brown coat with a hood drinking tea in the corner. The man, he was to say later, had laughing eyes, as if crinkled into a permanent smile. He has never been seen since.

When Linda did not come home her parents checked round every relative, every schoolfriend, everyone who would know her in their tight community, the library, the baker's yard, the cobbler's shop, the school, the church. There was no sign of her. So they went to the village policeman and he joined the search.

When it was clear that she was not at any known address and that she was not the kind of girl to stray because she was good and obedient and knew her mother needed a hand, the policeman was very concerned and called headquarters at Chelmsford. The head of the CID, Detective Chief Superintendent Jack Barkway, was also concerned. He had daughters of his own and although that was just a bonus to his judgement, any missing child was a matter of importance to police, particularly a girl of Linda's age.

The police were right to be so concerned but sadly were too late.

Three long days went by before there was any news of her. During that time Chief Superintendent Jack Barkway and the Essex team went through all the routine that starts any inquiry for a missing child: the questioning again and again of parents, relatives, friends and acquaintances to try to check every piece of knowledge they obtain during such interrogations, the hunt of the area where she might have gone, with officers on foot with dogs and the building up of an intricately detailed picture of the little girl, her habits, friends her parents might not know of, people she should not be speaking to or pets she might be keeping secretly at a friend's house.

The police came up with nothing. Everyone in the village wanted to help. They could not. Only the café proprietor had a lead and that went no further than a man with laughing eyes and a little girl well away from the village. The café was on the A131 Braintree to Chelmsford road.

The police hoped that what the café proprietor had seen was not a man and Linda, that it was not the little girl and her abductor. They were not sure that she had been abducted because her parents' protested that Linda would never accept a lift from a stranger, had had it drummed into her. What if it was not a stranger who had invited her into his car at five minutes past five?

As each day passed the fear grew and tragically but rightly so, because three days later farm worker John Richardson found what he thought was a bundle of old clothes lying in a clover field near his home at Polstead, Suffolk. It was a village some ten or eleven miles from Earls Colne and the field was very near the infamous Red Barn where William Corder murdered his lover Maria Marten in 1827 and was hanged at Bury St Edmunds shortly afterwards. The story has been written about all over the world either as a book or play.

Such historical information was of no interest to the detectives as they arrived. The bundle of clothes had proved on closer examination to be the body of Linda Smith, face down, her hood still up but one of her black lace-up shoes, size one, and her purse, missing. In one hand, tightly clutched, was the ten-shilling note her grandmother had given her to buy the paper.

She had been strangled with her school scarf. Dr Francis Camps, the famous Home Office pathologist, carried out the post-mortem and confirmed his initial diagnosis. There was no sign of sexual assault but detectives thought that was because the little girl had started to struggle while advances were being made and the killer, who might well have been known to her and been terrified that she would tell when she got home, silenced her forever.

The location of Polstead suggested local knowledge. To get there directly was a tortuous route along back roads and lanes through Bures and on to Honey Tye, crossing the A134 Sudbury–Colchester road and dropping down to Polstead. It was in exactly the opposite direction to Great Leighs but that did not rule out the sighting of the man with laughing eyes. He could well have gone back on his route if indeed he was the killer.

Forensic examination of the scene showed that she had lain there for three days, obviously dumped there the night she was snatched from the village street.

When the little girl's clothes were sent to Lewis Nickolls, director of the Metropolitan Police laboratory, he made a thorough search for anything that might help find the killer whose action had so incensed the villagers that at one stage they were seriously talking about a lynch party should he be caught.

Mr Nickolls found three small pieces of evidence that he would not normally expect to find on a schoolgirl's coat: wheat starch grains, some fragments of a red soluble lacquer paint in three layers – red, yellow, red – and fragments of another red paint, a single red insoluble lacquer. It naturally led to two questions: what was the paint and where had she got it from so that it stuck to her coat? He passed on the information to the two officers running the inquiry in Earls Colne, for as the body had been found in Suffolk, another county, they had called in Scotland Yard, something Essex never did.

At the scene forensic officers also found some heel prints too and casts were made. Mr Nickolls and the two senior detectives had a good look at them.

So now the police had something more to go on. They went to the village bakehouse on the High Street and saw the baker and other staff and asked if they had seen Linda that night. Gordon Jones the baker (not his real name), said that he had not because he normally arrived about six in the morning and left around four in the afternoon. He did not know Linda nor had he seen her but he knew that she had been round asking for tins and that might explain how starch came to be on her coat: that she had been shifting through the rubbish tip in the yard.

It took the investigation no further forward because it was quite possibly true. But there was still the question of the paint and Mr Nickolls was having great difficulty in identifying it. He contacted all the leading paint manufacturers but none of them could tell him where it came from. It certainly was not from their range. He kept on trying.

The police kept on trying too but without success. There was no trace of the man with the laughing eyes and there was no fresh evidence to help the inquiry along. It was one of those periods when police need a bit of luck with their perseverance. They got what looked like luck very quickly.

The baker worked on his own and travelled ten miles each day into work and then ten miles home. Police as part of the routine of a murder inquiry asked if they could look in his car and the 26-year-old baker agreed.

On the blanket on the back seat were fragments of white starch similar to the grain found on Linda's coat. There were also fragments of red paint, two different types of red paint, the same as those found on her coat, identical in size. When forensic experts took his overcoat to Mr Nickolls, the scientist found that on it were some white grains but also, though barely visible, some more fragments of red paint, the same two types. When a vacuum was run over the coat there were sixteen more, all the same shape, all the mysterious paint.

In Mr Nickolls's view they must have come from the same source.

It was quite a find but the police needed more than that before they started making accusations. There could be a logical explanation.

Detective Superintendent Jack Mannings who had been sent down by Scotland Yard, went to see the baker on nine occasions, interviewing him as a witness not a suspect. On 9 February, just over a fortnight after the murder, he saw him at the bakehouse and asked:

'You are quite sure you did not know Linda Smith?' and the handsome baker said:

'No, I did not know her and I have never seen her.'

'Do you know if she has ever been in the bakehouse?'

'Not to my knowledge.'

The superintendent asked, 'Have you ever seen her using the toilet in the yard?' and the answer was 'No'.

A day later the superintendent saw the baker twice, again asking him questions and again being given the same replies.

The next day the superintendent went out to the baker's house in a small village near Colchester. He lived there with his wife and they had been happily married for two and a half years. Two months earlier she had had a miscarriage and since then they had not had normal marital sex.

This time the police removed small articles, clothing and other items, from the baker's bungalow and they were sent to the Metropolitan Police laboratory for examination.

At the same time Detective Chief Inspector John McCafferty from the laboratory went to the bakehouse and went over it with a fine toothcomb in the presence of the baker. The policeman took sweepings from a pair of trousers and examined two raincoats hanging near the oven.

Then he went to the baker's home and vacuumed his wife's clothing and took away everything red in the house, red clothes, shoe polish, chair polish, red dusters, anything that might provide a clue and a link between the red fragments of paint which still had not been identified on Linda's coat and the baker's coat and blanket.

There was nothing further, nothing at all.

But once the laboratory had come up with the definite link between Linda and the baker Detective Superintendent Mannings went back to the baker again. This time it was in the police station at Sudbury where the baker went at the policeman's request.

Mannings said, 'Since seeing you last I have been informed by the police laboratory that they have found traces of flour and other substances not yet identified on Linda's clothing. These match substances on your clothing indicating the possibility of you having been in contact with the dead girl. I must tell you this in case there is an innocent explanation.'

The baker considered this and then asked, 'What sort of substances?'

The detective said, 'I don't know except that two are red and might look something like paint.'

The baker was puzzled. 'Paint? I can't remember getting paint on my clothes.'

Mannings told him: 'I cannot say they are paint. In addition to these substances being found on Linda's clothing and your clothing traces of some substances have been found in your car.'

The baker was nonchalant. 'Why tell me this anyway?' he asked.

The policeman explained. 'I am telling you this because Linda's movements were traced all along the High Street until she was within a few yards of your bakehouse and she was not seen again although several people who knew her were in the High Street at the time.'

The baker said nothing but sat quietly as the policeman went on, putting all that they knew to him.

'When her coat was examined a high concentration of wheat starch or flour was found so naturally we began checking on people like yourself who are associated with flour.

'The scientists also found the other substances I have mentioned and when they examined your clothes they not only found the flour as one would expect but also the same type of coloured substances they found on Linda's coat.'

There was a pause and then the baker said, 'I admit it looks serious but I could not have done it. I was not there.'

Superintendent Mannings had not finished. 'Are you sure you have not been in contact with her or that she has not been in your car?'

The baker was adamant. 'Not so far as I know. I know she has been asking for tins and the only theory that I can offer is that she was searching the rubbish dump near the incinerator and got the substances on her then.

'I use that rubbish dump and the substances from my clothes could have fallen off.'

That was his explanation. The police already had another pointer against the baker, another piece of evidence: his shoes. The heels of his shoes were the same size and shape as the impressions found round the area where Linda was dumped, shoe imprints next to the body. There were ten of them in the clover alongside a small handkerchief, a small piece of blue cloth, a Co-op mint and an empty whisky bottle, none of which had anything to do with the investigation.

There was enough evidence to start preparing a file to send to the Director of Public Prosecutions, who has to decide whether there is a prima-facie case strong enough to go to a jury for them to consider whether the person charged is guilty or not.

The fact that the fragments and the wheat grains had been found on both Linda's and the baker's clothing was very important indeed. The fact that similar pieces were on the blanket too was added weight to information that pointed at the baker. The fact that his bakery was so very close to the spot where the little girl was last seen alive was more evidence against him.

But he had two aids to help him. There was nothing from his home to link him any further with the paint and he had a reasonable explanation in saying that he used the rubbish dump and Linda could have gone on it. She might also have got into his car in the yard just to have a look. People did not have to lock their cars like they have to now.

But there was something else and vastly more important. He was at home when Linda set off for the paper shop, had been there for half an hour, was ready for his supper and even more, he had witnesses who could prove it. All that went into the set of statements from the police, the baker and other witnesses which were sent to the Director. It all took time and it was weeks after the murder before it went off.

While the Director was deciding what to do and the baker waiting to hear if he would be charged, Dale Parkinson, a big, forceful solicitor, stepped into the arena. He was rare in that he was a member of the Bar both in Britain and America. He was a powerful advocate and cross-examiner and had a practice in central London and in Sudbury. He went to see Linda's parents.

When the Director of Public Prosecutions decided there was insufficient evidence with which to charge anyone, Mr Smith, through Dale Parkinson, decided to seek a private warrant for the arrest of the baker on a charge of murdering his daughter.

The hearing lasted three and a half hours before a bench of four men and one woman behind closed doors in the red brick, cream-painted courthouse at Boxford, just three miles from the spot where Linda's body was found.

Mr Parkinson had a thirty-page dossier which included photographs and statements from two witnesses. He had conducted the interviews himself. He spent twenty-five minutes with the magistrates in the mushroom-painted courtroom. The magistrates spent over an hour reading the depositions as silver-haired Parkinson waited outside in the June sunshine.

Then they called in Superintendent Mannings who talked to them for half an hour. Then they asked Mr Parkinson to go back in and finally the magistrates – three farmers, a factory manager and the wife of a Congregational minister – opened the court to the press and the public and announced their decision.

The chairman, Colonel Kenneth Crockatt, read from a typewritten statement. It said: 'Certain evidence has been submitted to us by the informant, Mr Parkinson, and we have also had the advantage of hearing Detective Superintendent Mannings of Scotland Yard who is in charge of this case.

'After the most careful consideration of all relevant facts my fellow justices and I – we are unanimous – wish to state that we are not satisfied that there is sufficient prima-facie evidence in support of the information which has been laid and the application for a warrant is accordingly refused.'

Mr Parkinson immediately announced to the press that he would advise the Smiths to apply to a judge in chambers within twenty-four hours for a warrant which meant an appeal against the magistrates' decision. It did not happen because four days later the full inquest on the little girl started in the same court and went on for two days in front of Coroner Thomas Wilson, a solicitor of the old school who stood no nonsense from anyone whom he did not like; even if he did like them he made sure all the facts came out. But it was he who would decide which facts were relevant.

It was a fascinating inquest in which the baker was really on trial. If the jury took the view that the evidence against him was overwhelming they could commit him for trial on a charge of murder. No private warrant would be needed then.

The baker took his wife with him and sat in the waiting room with the dead girl's parents. The inquest had already been opened and adjourned so that Linda could be buried. The evidence then was simply identification by her father and the medical evidence that she had died by strangulation.

Now the inquest resumed with a jury of nine men. Once they were sworn in the coroner called the Director of the Metropolitan Police laboratory, Lewis Nickolls.

The baker was in court but his wife waited outside as Nickolls told how he found the matching wheat starch grains and the two different types of paint fragments on Linda's coat and on the baker's coat and car blanket but despite taking eighty-six items from the house, on no other.

He said, 'This indicates in my experience that they were derived from the same source while their position on the garments suggests some kind of contact between them.'

Dale Parkinson, who was representing Linda's father, asked:

'There are three specific items of forensic evidence which directly link Linda and him?' Nickolls was an old hand and was not going to say anything that he could not prove definitely. He replied:

'I'd rather say there are three items that are on Linda's clothing which are on his overcoat and blankets.

'I did not find the paint anywhere else. I did find wheat starch on other articles but only with people associated with the bakehouse where he worked.'

He said that the two types of paint were sufficiently rare for him to try to find out their source but he had not been able to do so. In fact, no one has ever been able to identify them.

They were, Nickolls said, after further examination, transient material which no longer exist at the scene of the crime.

The solicitor representing the baker, Mr Christopher Lubbock, said he could not ask any questions at that stage because the evidence was new to him and he had not had any chance of considering its relevance to his client. He asked for an adjournment but the coroner would allow only half an hour because the Director had to give evidence in an assize court case the next day in Hampshire and that took precedence.

After the half-hour break Mr Lubbock again repeated his request but the coroner was adamant that there would be no adjournment so Mr Lubbock said he had no questions and the next witness, Detective Chief Inspector McCafferty, was called.

He told of all the sweepings and clothings he took at the bakehouse, in the car, from clothing and from the baker's house, 'everything which could have been the source of this red material'.

Mr Lubbock asked: 'Red shoe polish?'

'Yes.'

'Red chair?'

'Yes.'

'All red clothes?'

'No,' he had found nothing.

Then Dr Camps told how Linda died from strangulation with her school scarf. Mr Parkinson asked how she was strangled and Dr Camps said, 'With a firm deliberate pull from the right side and possibly behind.'

Parkinson: 'If she was sitting in a car with the driver on her right side could it happen like that?'

'Yes,' Camps replied.

Then the butchery manager at the Co-op where Jones was the baker told how he saw the baker driving towards Colchester away from the village on the day that Linda vanished, at five minutes past four and how the baker honked his horn and put his hand up.

Dale Parkinson leapt into the attack. First he asked the butchery manager if he and the baker were good friends and was told they only knew each other through work.

Parkinson then suggested that the baker had approached the manager about the car incident, which the latter said he had not. He had first read of Linda's disappearance on 18 January, the Wednesday, and when he mentioned it to the baker he did not show any surprise.

'How many times did you discuss this girl with this man?' Parkinson demanded.

'I did not again.'

'He never suggested to you that this would be a jolly good alibi for him?'

'No,' the butchery manager replied and then Mr Lubbock asked him:

'Is what you have told the coroner a pack of lies to help the baker or the whole truth?'

'The whole truth.'

Linda's father Robert was next and he said she was a very friendly and rather inquisitive girl but he had never known her to take car rides. Her mother sent her shopping but he did not know whether she ever went to the baker for bread and buns.

One of her sisters, aged eleven, said she had been in the baker's yard and had been in the bakery and asked the man for something but then her answers became inaudible and she became frightened, clutching at her mother who sat beside her.

The coroner asked Mr Lubbock if the baker would stand up so the little girl could identify him but Mr Lubbock was firm. He said:

'My client is obviously known throughout the village and is in a difficult position and I think it would be very wrong to ask this child a question which may do him great damage when she is of such tender years.'

The coroner took his point and said he would not pursue the matter, telling the jury of villagers:

'My view is that the witness is very shaky about a great many points and you cannot attach very much importance to her evidence.'

There were other witnesses like her, a great aunt who said she was a simple, happy trusting child without an enemy in the world, a schoolfriend who saw her outside the newsagent when she went in but not when she came out and the cobbler who said she had asked him for some tins on the evening she disappeared but he had none. He said he had never seen her go into the yard at the back of the Co-op.

There the coroner adjourned for the day and everyone went out into the sunshine and got quietly into their cars to drive home. The press who had packed the benches in the small court went to a nearby hotel to write their stories of the day's proceedings. The inquest had attracted a great deal of interest following the application a few days before for the warrant on behalf of the parents.

What the Smiths said to each other that night, what the baker and his wife discussed, we do not know but they were all back the next morning when the policeman leading the inquiry and the baker were to give evidence.

The policeman was the first witness. He told the coroner and the jury, all in their best suits, how he had nine interviews with the baker and took five statements from him. The coroner asked:

'None of the statements was made under caution?'

'It would have been wrong to caution the man,' the superintendent said.

'Why?' The coroner, like everyone else, was curious.

'He was a witness as far as I was concerned. I had no intention of making any arrest on the evidence available to me.'

'You had no intention of making any charge against him?' the coroner asked. He wanted to be sure.

'No sir,' the policeman replied.

'And you have not done so since?' The coroner wanted ratification.

'No, sir.'

Then he told of the interviews he had with the baker, the conversations he had, the replies he had got. He told how the baker denied any knowledge of the girl and how he could not explain how the starch and the paint came to be on the clothing nor what the paint was.

When the policeman had finished his main evidence Mr Lubbock asked him if he had been present on the previous Friday when the magistrates refused the application by the father for a warrant for the arrest of a man for her murder. The policeman said he had been.

'Was it clear that the magistrates were deliberating about whether a warrant should be issued for the arrest of my client?'

'Yes,' said the policeman.

'Have you laid before the Director of Public Prosecutions all the information you have given the coroner today?' Superintendent Mannings said that was so and the information included Mr Nickolls's report.

Mr Lubbock asked if eighty-six items that the baker owned or might have come into contact with had been taken away. Mannings replied: 'I have not totted them up but there was a very large number.'

But when Dale Parkinson asked if it was correct that the magistrates had none of the scientific evidence the coroner cut him short by saying:

'I shall tell the jury to pay no attention whatsoever to whether the magistrates turned down this application or not.'

Parkinson asked if the policeman had questioned the baker about his shoes. He had and the baker had confirmed that the shoes were the ones he was wearing on the day Linda disappeared.

Before calling the baker the coroner read out the statements made by him to the police including the one in which he said that on the night the little girl vanished he got home around half past four and never went out again, and how he was happily married.

Then the smartly suited dark-haired baker went into the witness box to give his own account in front of the jury.

He was a handsome young man, assured, pleasant. He took the oath and the coroner said:

'You must understand I would not call you unless you did not want to give evidence. Do you want to give evidence?'

Without hesitation he said, 'Yes' firmly.

Outside the sun was shining and the birds were singing their songs into a clear blue sky. No one in the courtroom was listening or thinking about the outside world. They wanted to hear what this young man would say in answer to an unspoken charge of abducting a little girl off a village street and strangling her and dumping her body in a field over the border into Suffolk.

There was no hesitation when he answered questions. The coroner told him that if he thought any question he was asked would incriminate him, he did not have to answer. But the baker did not use this right. He wanted everyone to know that he was not the killer of the little girl. It was a terrible position that he was in and he and everyone else knew it. But was he the killer?

He started by saying that on the Monday she vanished he got to work at six in the morning and was working on his own in the bakery all day. He went on:

'I generally leave between 3.45 p.m. and 4 p.m. and on that day I left at approximately the same time. I went straight home arriving about half an hour later. I didn't go out again that day.

'I put my car in the garage. My wife was at home. I believe there was one of her friends there with a baby but I am not sure.

'My brother Norman came to the house between five and a quarter past. It was the usual thing for him to do on a Monday and Tuesday at about that time. He has a meal and goes back to Colchester for technical college evening classes.'

So he was at home when Linda vanished. If his evidence was true. If it was, then he could not have killed her.

The coroner asked: 'Did you know this girl Linda Smith?' The baker was emphatic when he said 'No'.

'When you left on 16 January was there anyone in the bakery except you?'

'Not when I left.'

On his way home, he went on, he saw the butchery manager and said, 'He saw me, I know that, because he put his hand up.'

He said he had not been out of the bakehouse all day and when he left he did not see a little girl standing on the pavement.

The coroner turned to the paint. 'Can you account in any way for these red particles that were found on your clothing?'

'No,' came the reply without pause.

What about the girl? The coroner asked the question directly:

'Did you when you left take any little girl with you?'

The baker looked straight ahead and said firmly, 'No sir.'

The coroner asked another direct question. 'Can you give us any help as to how and where this girl met her death?' Again there was no waiting.

'No sir,' came the reply, firmly and clear.

'You say you know nothing about her and her death?' the coroner asked, pressing the point so that there would be no ambiguity.

'That's correct, sir, that's right.' Just as straight as the question.

'Can you suggest at all how these particles or similar particles were found both on your coat and this girl's coat?' The baker was definite.

'I only had one guess, sir, and I gave that to the police.'

'Can you suggest how it was that a considerable amount of flour was found on her coat?''

'Well sir, there are several reasons but none relating to me.'

That was it. The coroner asked him no more. Dale Parkinson wanted to ask questions and did so but without shaking the baker at all.

The final witness was the baker's brother, Norman, who was eighteen. He said that he was working in Colchester and when he finished work at five he went straight to his brother's bungalow about a mile and a half away on his motorbike.

He said, 'When I got there he was sitting in a chair. His wife was there as well.'

He stayed there he said until 6.15 p.m., having his tea and then went to evening class in Colchester.

When he had finished – and there were no questions – Dale Parkinson said that he was willing to go into the witness box and give evidence of the statements the baker had made to him. It was not to be.

The coroner said sharply, 'I don't think that would be necessary or desirable.' Instead he turned to the jury of Suffolk men good and true and summed up, telling them:

'It is only right that this should have been a very full investigation. This was a terrible crime. We all feel the person responsible should be brought to justice.

'The medical evidence is clear. She was strangled with her own scarf. What evidence is there to connect anybody with the death of this girl? There is no doubt that this little girl had at some time gone to use the lavatory in the bakery yard. There is no evidence that she did on this occasion.

'The baker could see quite well into the yard from his bakery. When samples were taken from the clothing of this girl it was found there was flour and some red particles on her clothing. The particles were also found on some of the baker's clothing.

'The mere fact there was flour on her I think doesn't make conclusive evidence that there was any contact between the baker and this little girl.'

But, he went on, the red particles presented a different problem. What was the explanation for how they came on to both sets of clothing without contact?

'You have got to attach to it such weight as you think right. Do these particles or some other evidence point to the baker as being the man who killed this little girl?'

He had, the coroner observed, been interviewed by the police on many occasions.

'I think it's for you to say that he doesn't appear from his statements – and he didn't appear to me today – to be a man who was hiding a lot.'

And there was another thing in his favour, the fact that the butchery manager and his wife saw the baker going home at five minutes past four. Although it had been suggested the story had been concocted between the two men it was in fact the butcher who had told the police, not the baker.

That was it. The butcher and the brother said they saw him in situations where he could not have possibly been the man who murdered Linda. But the baker had the particles of the paint on his clothes. So had Linda. That was the only link and if the two men who placed the baker miles from the scene when she was taken were telling the truth, and there was absolutely no reason to doubt that they were, then there was another explanation for the particles getting on the clothes of both of them.

It took the jury just twenty minutes to say that it was not the baker who killed her but some person unknown.

The baker and his wife went out into the sunlight. So too did the Smiths.

Nothing has happened over the years to change the situation from that moment late on the afternoon of 21 June 1961.

There has been no additional evidence, no one has come forward to say they saw a car stop and pick Linda up that night, that they know who did, that the killer confessed to them because he could no longer bear the strain of that dreadful secret that he took the girl and killed her because he could not face the consequences when she told what he tried to do. No one has made a death-bed confession.

It may well be that the murderer is dead, dying in prison serving a sentence for an attack on another girl. It could be that the strangler was a man who had done it before, had no compunction about doing it another time and could live with it.

Or it may be that the man has nightmares and one day they will become too strong to live with and then he will have to tell, to get it off his conscience so that he can sleep and come to some kind of peace with himself.

Whatever the truth is, whoever did it, two things are certain: the baker did not do it and no one has ever been able to identify the paint or where it came from.

It is almost unbelievable in this hi-tech age.

6

Maffia

The Magpie Mystery

Tony Maffia was an East End boy who made very good in the underworld in the 1960s, a man whom the police would dearly have loved to put behind bars because he was one of the biggest fences in London, but they were never able to prove it, at least while he was alive. The only time he went to prison was for helping in the escape of a man from custody in the law courts in London. His other activities were suspected and probed but never proved. There was just no evidence and Maffia was clever.

He had two nicknames and they were names by which he was actually known, not like so many where someone is dubbed or nicknamed some ridiculous title that lasts for a few moments. Maffia was known as the Magpie because he bought or collected anything and anything in his case could mean a watch or a collection of stolen gold or priceless antiques. He was also known as the Fox because he was so sharp and smart in business and because of his skill in never letting his right hand know what his left was doing.

He moved in rich circles and had a yacht and nice house and was also known for his meanness among his friends. Most of his life was spent officially in the motor trade, running a genuine business in the East End with different partners including his wife until they broke up, and he had business interests in a copper mine and a hotel in Jersey.

That was what the world saw, the successful businessman moving in top financial circles. Behind the outer skin was the real Maffia, a high-quality fence through whom much of the big crime of the sixties passed. Shortly before his death on 27 May 1968, he had shown an interest in forged bank notes, some of which were offered to him by a man from Manchester with whom he had become friendly during his prison sentence in 1957 which he served in Stafford jail.

Maffia had gone to Belgium a few days before his death and his contacts there had examined some forged ten shilling and ten pound notes which he had with him (and no one knows where they came from) and told him he might have been conned. The Magpie was not at all pleased and with his feathers ruffled he returned to London.

On the day he died the mean Magpie was up early because his old friend from Manchester was coming to London and was talking about buying Maffia's forty-foot twin-diesel, six-berth cruiser *Calamara* which was moored at a marina at Wallasea Island, Essex, a bit south of the Triangle, where he was a member of the yacht club.

The man was Steve Jewell, a 45-year-old coal merchant, who in the months before Maffia's murder had met him a few times, initially to discuss some forged ten pound notes Jewell had obtained from a man in a Salford Casino. This man had offered the coal merchant, who had once dabbled in club running, first option on £32,000 worth of forged tenners for £8,000 real cash. Two days before Maffia died Jewell was rung at home (to which he objected) by Maffia and told to bring another forged tenner. When he made the call Maffia was with two associates and they all agreed that Jewell was 'a right idiot'. According to Jewell later on, on the same day he had another call during which Maffia told him to bring a pistol with him as he was having trouble with someone. Jewell did as he was told, bringing a .22 Browning automatic.

He came south the next day, providing the tenuous but threefold link with the Triangle itself. He travelled through it to make his way to London; when Maffia's death was discovered extensive inquiries were made in the Triangle in case his killer was one of his many customers whom he may have cheated; thirdly, Chief

Inspector John McCafferty who has been mentioned in other cases in the Triangle, became involved too.

Shortly after nine Jewell arrived at Maffia's house in Buckhurst Hill, east London, and liked it so much that he expressed an interest in buying it. It was on the market following Maffia's marital problems for £12,000 which was a lot in those days. Jewell also looked at the information about the £20,000 cruiser and they discussed one of the forged notes that Jewell had brought with him.

Soon after, Jewell insisted on going to the marina with Maffia accompanying him which annoyed the fence not a little. They went in Maffia's green Jaguar with the splendid registration number MCC 932, which had a towbar for his speed boat. Jewell took his gun with the special ammunition – a hole in the nose of every round – on Maffia's orders and loaded it before getting in the car for the trip down to Essex. He put the gun on the front seat between them and the magazine with a piece of cloth over them. He left his own car in the car-park of a pub near Maffia's home.

After looking at the boat and having a drink at the marina they headed back towards London, but not until Maffia had made a reverse-charge call to his partner to say he would be back in an hour or so and telling the manager at the marina that he did not think Jewell would buy the boat because he did not have that kind of money.

What happened on the road back to London from Essex will never really be known. Jewell's version was that as they came up the road from the marina they were forcibly stopped by three men in a Ford Zodiac who made Maffia get out of the Jaguar. They wanted to talk to him about some deal and told Jewell to get lost and take a walk back towards the marina. He did so and when he returned a little later the men, Maffia and the Zodiac had gone but the Jaguar was still there. Instead of his overcoat neatly hiding the pistol, it was blood-stained and the pistol and ammo had gone.

He was not sure what to do but in the end he got behind the wheel of the Jaguar and set off for London on a road he did not know. He stopped after ten miles to throw his stained overcoat over a hedge and drove on.

When the overcoat was found because a retired master plasterer saw him wipe the bottom of the passenger door with it before throwing it over a hedge, police found a live .22 bullet and an estate agent's handout for Maffia's home and boat among other items. The coat was a raglan Crombie, given to Jewell by his mother ten years earlier.

After that he dumped the green Jaguar in the car-park of the Midway Restaurant, named because it is half way between London and Southend on the A127. He then hitched a lift back to London and to his car in the pub car-park before driving back to Manchester. That night in a Charlton, Manchester, club he told one of the stewards about his trip to south and how men in a white Jaguar had stopped him and his colleague 'who had been clobbered' and gone off but that he had left his coat behind in the car.

He was not to mention the incident again until Saturday, 1 June, and by that time the number of men and the car involved had been changed and he had had a threatening phone call. His acquaintance, Jewell said for the first time, was Maffia.

Maffia never made it back to London, whatever had happened to him.

His colleagues had reported him missing but there was no trace of him until mid morning on the Whit Holiday Saturday, 1 June, when one of the staff at the restaurant saw a dog sniffing at a green Jaguar which had been parked in the same position by the fence of the car-park since 27 May. The man went to have a look and saw a blue tarpaulin over the passenger seat. The window was slightly open and he managed to force the door and when he got it open the stench hit him like a blow to the solar plexus. He forced himself to lift the tarpaulin and saw a man's feet.

They belonged – as police and forensic experts quickly discovered – to the late Magpie whose body was bloated in the heat and could only be identified by a fingerprint from his criminal record card and by a gold ring he always wore.

Tests showed that he had been shot twice, once by the right eye and the second behind the right ear, probably by someone standing outside the offside window of the green Jag, the shots blowing Maffia across the seat and into the well in front of the passenger seat. Whether he had landed in the position in which he was found or whether he had been given a push to land him on the floor no one knows.

However, he had been missing for four days in a car with the distinctive MCC number plate and now the hunt was on for the killer. The field of those who might have done it was big but Steve Jewell stopped the search almost as soon as it started. He told his friend in Manchester that he had been threatened and asked him to call the police on his behalf.

In the early hours of 3 June Jewell met detectives and later that day the man in charge of the case, Detective Chief Superintendent Kenneth Drury of the Murder Squad on his first murder outside London, and other officers flew north and brought Jewell back.

Drury, who was later head of the Flying Squad and then disgraced before his death, had insisted on team work throughout the inquiry and that was how the investigation had started and went on. He and his top men listened as Jewell told them his story about coming to London and going to the marina and the men who had taken Maffia away and how he had dumped the Jaguar and hitched a lift back to the pub, although he was not at all sure how he got there. He said that he was innocent of the murder and that he and his family had received threatening phone calls and even a letter.

The evidence against him was strong, particularly from eye-witnesses who put him with Maffia after he had left the marina, the man who had seen him throw away his overcoat on which forensic experts found part of Maffia's brains and the fingerprints on the car including the rear bumper suggesting he had opened the boot to take out the tarpaulin.

When he came to trial he had different details for the men and car that stopped them and where and the jury did not believe him; he was convicted of murder by a majority verdict of ten to two and sentenced to life without any recommendation of the term he should serve.

But even in custody Jewell insisted he was not the killer.

There was no real motive for him to kill the Magpie, no hint of why he did it; when was the moment when he decided to do it and why should he take such a terrible chance and then, having gone back to Manchester, go to the police? Was it to clear his name in the hope that his story (whatever version of the original it was) would be believed? Even his own counsel was to describe him as a pathological liar.

But although the police could not put their finger on what caused him to die they certainly uncovered a great deal about the Magpie and files that had stood unused about major robberies over the past decade were taken down and opened again when they unlocked the safe deposit boxes that Maffia rented.

The trail started when they emptied his pockets in the mortuary after his brother had identified him by the gold solitaire ring he wore. In the pockets were cash and cheques worth around £700 together with two gold 1931 mint sovereigns and other coins. It was then that police knew that robbery was not the motive which made his murder even more of a puzzle.

In his boxes they found a collection of rare coins stolen in a Middlesex robbery and worth around £100,000. Maffia was an expert on coins. There was a gold bar cut into eighteen pieces, worth around £25,000 and when the pieces were put together they represented almost one whole gold bar stolen in a 140-bar haul taken during the £750,000 Rothschild gold bullion robbery from a van in 1967 in Bowling Green Lane, east London.

There were thousands of mint gold sovereigns, most of them still in their Swiss bank wrappers and many, many more coins from nearly forty different countries. Most of them belonged to Maffia, being part of his collection, and went into his estate which was worth over £80,000.

There was also a wonderful collection of stamps including 1,396 faulty 3d ones worth £10 each and art treasures such as miniature Dresden figures, diamond rings, gold rings and bracelets and other jewellery.

Most of the hoard was put on show and some pieces in the strong box collection worth around £250,000 (and over a million in 1990) were recognized by those from whom they had been stolen. But the bulk of the collection belonged to Maffia himself and was auctioned and the proceeds – after the taxman and other interested parties had had their cut – went to his estate.

One part of the Maffia Magpie collection that did not go on show were the stolen rare coins. They were claimed by their rightful owner, a Surrey stockbroker who was recognized as a leading authority on 'hammered' coins ranging from the seventh to fourteenth centuries. His collection was valued at £100,000 and the British Museum only had plaster casts of some of his coins. They had been stolen two years before Maffia received the final part of his hoard – two bullets in the head – and only twenty had been recovered before the Magpie died. His death meant the return of all but a handful of the wonderful collection of English history stretching from the Saxons into the fourteenth century.

The hoard that Maffia kept so secret was in boxes found at banks in Forest Gate, Mayfair and in the City of London. But were there more in other names and did the friends who Maffia always kept at arm's length have any idea what names he might have used? Police doubted it but it was another mystery in what is a baffling case even now.

It left so many questions unanswered:

Why did Jewell kill him? No satisfactory explanation has ever been given. There have been theories, that Jewell shot him because he would not join a forgery racket or invest in another club venture that Jewell was so keen to start, that Jewell was a hitman ordered to gun down the Magpie because he was swindling the men for whom he acted as fence. Jewell has insisted without deviation that he had nothing to do with the killing, that he was a man who knew and befriended Maffia in prison and had come to buy his yacht before three other men took his friend away to kill him for reasons not known. The jury did not believe him but he has never altered his version.

But a fence Maffia certainly was and as police probed after the killing they discovered that he was probably the biggest in the country. The ingot came from one of the biggest gold bullion robberies in history up to that time and the thieves had to know someone who could get rid of the extremely valuable loot. The rare coins were a major theft too and the thieves had to know where to move them. Maffia was known to have the contacts who could shift, export, move round the world the rare commodities that he bought in. He also had money which meant that he could hold on to items for as long as was necessary, which could often be years, until the right buyer came along who would pay the price and would be delighted to have such a rare item even if it was stolen, to add to his own collection, a rarity that only he could admire but a rarity that only he would want to admire.

There was no proof of other property that he had handled but police estimated it ran well into seven figures. There was also his currency trading in Britain and abroad and his dabbling in forged notes. As he did not tell anyone what he was up to, often pleaded poverty and was known as an extremely mean man who would sell a stolen ring just to buy the drinks, the police were never able fully to unravel what he had been up to.

But the problem was compounded by the fact that his front businesses were genuine. He was a motor trader, he did have an interest in a copper mine and these dealings were kosher.

It was just another shade of a mystery that will never be solved.

7

Bull

Millionaire Wife-Killer

Coggeshall is a village full of antique shops. Some places have a lot of pubs, others boutiques and trendy bric-à-brac but Coggeshall is famous for its antique shops, so proud that it advertises itself on the main A130 road as 'Antiques + Coggeshall' so that anyone passing along the road who is interested in antiques will turn off right down the main street and into the market area where they abound like trees.

The Bull family had a good business. It was growing. The two brothers, Wilfred and David, looked set to make the thriving business a great success. Wilfred was charming, David equally pleasant and courting a girl called Patsy back in 1961, when there was a serious blip in their lives.

On a cold, frosty December morning the two brothers had gone out to shoot pheasants. It was Christmas time and the fields were full of birds who could provide good sport in the Essex countryside.

Wilfred and David took the guns out and went striding into the morning under clear blue skies with a severe bite in the air.

They took a few shots without hitting anything. They strode along breathing in the air so fresh that there were no germs, no modern pollution, just perfection on a wonderful morning that made both feel good to be alive. No man could ask for anything more at that moment in his life.

Then they came to a culvert and twenty-five years on Wilfred could remember exactly what happened. He said,

'There was a brick culvert and my brother jumped across. As I handed him his gun he slipped on the ice and fell back.

'I tried to save him but the gun went off and blew off the top of his head. This is something I have never been able to forget.'

He had the appalling task of trying to save his brother, of racing back to fetch help, to see if anyone else could do anything. No one could. Wilfred was inconsolable and so was David's girlfriend Patsy, a plumpish jolly girl who was full of life.

The terrible tragedy drew them together. They were together when the inquest was held and Wilfred had to give his account of what had happened. A verdict of accidental death was recorded and Wilfred and Patsy were at David's funeral.

Because of the death Wilfred inherited his brother's share of the family business and not too long afterwards his girlfriend too. Death brought them so close together that they married and had two children.

From the beginning their business partnership worked well and their reputation grew. They were experts in carvings and ivory figures and chairs. Among their customers over the years were Royalty, including Princess Margaret, and the then prime minister Harold Wilson. Customers came from all over Britain and from abroad too to their shop in the Essex village and they were a favourite haunt of Americans.

It was not all success. Wilfred became ill and they went to a specialist who diagnosed leukaemia. It was a disease from which victims rarely recovered and his chances of living were very slim. But Patsy was not having that. She took him to specialists everywhere. Each one examined him and each tried their best. As the hunt for someone to save him, and that meant save his life, went on he turned a brownish colour as if he had been under a sun lamp or been living in a sunny country for some time. Eventually they found a specialist who could cure his particular kind of leukaemia and he recovered and continued to live a normal life. The tan never went.

They were a good team, Patsy as bubbly and vivacious

as her husband was calm and serious. The money began to roll in and Patsy ran a high-class boutique with a friend who was also a fine hunt jockey. Dresses cost over £1,000.

Then came another setback. They had a superb mansion home and spent a great deal of money on renovating it. But a builder's blow-lamp caused a fire which did around £1,000,000 worth of damage. They were heartbroken but instead of continuing to bemoan their bad luck they set about having it rebuilt and it was.

But while this was happening, Wilfred was carrying on with a girl called Carol whom he met in late 1979. He was infatuated and obsessed with her. He could not take his eyes or his hands off her. Their affair grew but he kept it a secret for some years swearing friends to secrecy for he did not want to upset his wife.

Inevitably she found out and they had a terrible row which ended when he promised never to see Carol again. It was a promise he did not keep and he carried on the affair with subterfuge and lies and the help of some friends who covered for him.

For over a year Wilfred and Carol, twelve years his junior, continued their affair. And then, because she overheard him phoning her to make a date, Patsy discovered it was still on, that her husband was two-timing her despite all his promises. She was sick at heart, angry and very hurt. She caught him out trying to make a date at a champagne party on May Bank Holiday Monday 1985 which they were throwing for a few friends in their antique showroom in Coggeshall.

Wilfred kept going to the phone but could not raise Carol. Patsy could not help but notice and then she listened as she walked in on the call.

When the guests had gone she tackled him and threatened divorce.

Wilfred went home on his own. He told his son Charles that his mother was locking up the shop. A little while later Wilfred telephoned a friend with whom they were going out that night and said that Patsy was in the bath up to her arms in suds.

They were, said the man with the perpetual suntan, off on the Orient Express in a few days' time to celebrate

Patsy's forty-eighth birthday.

It was not a holiday date that would be kept. A little while later their teenage son Charles was worried that his mother had not come home and drove down to the shop to see what was keeping her. He did not know of the row although he knew of the affair and how unhappy his mother was about it. She had said earlier in the day that she suspected Wilfred was still seeing another woman.

The scene that Charles saw when he went into the shop made him turn away in fear, shock and revulsion. There in the storeroom where £500,000 worth of antiques were stored, lay the body of his mother, her head covered in blood.

Money was missing from the safe and police were called at once. Wilfred who had offered a £5,000 reward just a few weeks before after vandals smashed a valuable statue outside the shop was told by his son and was inconsolable. He collapsed and wept. When he recovered slightly he insisted on going down to the warehouse behind the shop to see for himself.

By that time the pathologist had been called and photographs taken of Patsy as she lay in a great pool of blood on the floor. The police's first impression was that she had died in a fall, perhaps even accidentally. They were not at first able to confirm theft because although there appeared to have been a robbery it was by no means certain. It was equally possible that she had opened the safe and had been up the storeroom ladder looking at stock when she fell and cracked her head open on the corner of the desk.

The body was taken to Colchester and a post-mortem was carried out some sixteen hours after her death. Once the blood was washed off the pathologist could see quite clearly how she had died.

There was a bullet from a .38 Smith and Wesson revolver embedded in her head. She had been shot from close range and it was a case of murder.

Police had several theories to consider. She could have been shot when she disturbed burglars and there was certainly around £2,000 missing from the safe. Her distraught husband had confirmed this when he went to the warehouse again.

That seemed the most likely answer but there could have been a domestic reason. In any case where a wife is involved and the actual reason for her murder is not immediately apparent or not quite right – often the case in a domestic shooting or killing – the first person the police investigate and interrogate is the husband. It is common sense that they should do so. He might be, and often is, totally innocent and it is only right that he should be cleared from the inquiry as quickly as possible. Or he may be implicated in some way: another woman on the scene, an attempt to frighten his wife off a lover which goes wrong, a hired killer coming in to remove a troublesome wife who is objecting to an affair, a killing that goes wrong and was never intended. All these things are considered by senior detectives. They were in the case of Patsy Bull and her distraught husband, inconsolable, under sedation in his grief.

The usual routine inquiries were made about Wilfred Bull. They turned up a crock of bad gold for the police who were, at the same time, looking for a gang of burglars who had a black Golf or Escort or Fiesta, the kind of car which was seen to turn in the Bulls' driveway shortly after the time police believed that Patsy was shot.

For a start, among the several firearms he had for protection was a .38 Smith and Wesson revolver. Then there was the death of his brother when his shotgun accidentally went off all those years ago. On top of that there were whispers that Wilfred Bull had a girlfriend, a friendship that was talked of openly, a girl who had a slightly wild reputation for her behaviour at parties which she always denied very strongly. There was too Bull's behaviour when the police went to his house. He opened the door to them wearing a suit which was dripping wet.

He explained to their astonishment that he had not realized he was dressed while he was taking a shower. They initially put it down to his grief, that he did not act normally because of the shock of his wife's death.

The papers were full of the murder for two reasons: two years earlier Diane Jones, the wife of the village's GP – and the Bulls were patients – was murdered and her killer never found. The hunt for her attacker is still going on.

The other reason was that the Bulls were internationally famous for their antiques with Royalty and VIPs as customers and their social connections were high. A friend of Patsy's said:

'I just can't believe it. It's absolutely shattering. It's the third tragedy to hit them in such a short time, the death of his brother, the house burning down, Wilfred's illness.

'She was so good at everything she turned her hand to. She and Wilfred had a marvellous business, she was in partnership in a high-class dress shop and she worked tirelessly for charity. She's only just helped raise £5,000 for a trust for a local hospital.'

The papers showed photographs of the couple with Harold Wilson and recalled their triumphs.

By this time the police had discovered a lot more about Wilfred's friendship with Carol. As papers printed another picture – that of them with Princess Margaret at a trade fair – the police went to talk to the two-timing husband about his affair and what his wife knew about it. They already knew that she did know about it but had accepted her husband's word that it was all over. Had she now discovered that it was still on, that he had been deceiving her?

This time Bull said, he would tell them the truth. He had been having an affair with Carol and he had told his wife it was over. But after the party she tackled him about it. It happened when he had one of the guns he kept for protection in case of robbery out of the drawer in his desk. It was the .38 Smith and Wesson and it was wrapped in a pair of women's tights.

She grabbed at them, Bull said, demanding to know whose they were and in that moment the gun went off and killed her and he panicked.

He was arrested. He went with police to his home to show them the gun. It was under the floorboards by a small safe and covered with gold ingots.

On the next day, 8 May 1985, Bull appeared before Chelmsford magistrates and was remanded in custody. He said nothing during the half-hour hearing. His son and daughter had also been arrested but after interviews were allowed to go with no accusation or suspicion against them.

A few days later a security firm was called in to guard the

Bulls' mansion after a burglar was spotted on the first floor. And at the end of the month Wilfred sent a wreath from his prison cell to his wife's funeral. The red roses had a note which said: 'Patsy I am totally lost without you. Love forever, Wilfred.'

It was six months before Bull tasted freedom again. He managed to raise the £650,000 bail, putting up £250,000 himself and two business friends raising the rest.

Six months later Bull was tried at the Old Bailey, away from his home county. He pleaded not guilty to the murder of his wife and sat, a heavily suntanned international expert on ivory and a millionaire, to hear the opening address to the jury by Mr William Denny QC.

It was a strange and compellingly awful story that he told. He alleged quite simply that Wilfred murdered his wife, faked it as a robbery and then 'cruelly and callously' pretended to friends within minutes that she was up to the arms in bubbles in her bath and they were planning to go on the Orient Express to celebrate her forty-eighth birthday. He even pretended to call her to the phone to one friend while knowing that she was lying dead in the warehouse.

The prosecutor asked: 'How can that callous presentation possibly square with the protestations of a supposedly distraught husband who had accidentally shot his wife?'

He said that Wilfred was seen by friends as a caring and affectionate father and husband but when in drink he could be quite different and vicious to his wife.

Later, when questioned by police he admitted he was having an affair and, the prosecutor alleged, when his wife found out she threatened divorce. Bull then confessed he had killed his wife but said that it was an accident when she grabbed at the gun.

The prosecutor suggested that in fact Bull murdered his wife because divorce would have meant splitting his fortune with her and he could not stand the thought of losing his cosy existence. He wanted to keep everything – his business, his mansion, his wife and his mistress.

Mr Denny alleged: 'Divorce would have been disastrous. It would have meant dividing everything.'

His son was one of the witnesses. He said that some time earlier when he was still at school he and his mother drove to a flat in Chelmsford where they found Wilfred and Carol. The son said:

'My mother threw Carol to the floor and pulled her hair. Then I took my mother away. It was a most unpleasant situation.'

Several years later he found his mother dead in the storeroom. Earlier that day she had seemed upset because she thought Wilfred was seeing Carol again.

When his father saw his mother's body he became hysterical and cried, 'Oh my God, Patsy.' The son said he had to restrain him and later on his father told him he had been so upset that he took a shower with his clothes on.

When the police began to give evidence of Patsy's murder Wilfred could not stand it and collapsed in the dock. He had to be helped when he began to sob.

He sobbed again when he gave his own evidence. He was telling how he accidentally shot Patsy when the revolver he was carrying went off by mistake.

'I thought "Oh my darling Patsy my life is in turmoil. This can't happen to me a second time."

'I was thinking of the tragedy with my brother.'

He said that as his wife lay dying at his feet, bleeding heavily from the bullet hole in her head, the accident with his brother 'flashed across my mind like a TV film'. The action replay stopped him from going to her aid.

He said: 'I was moving a pistol from the showroom. The gun was wrapped in a pair of tights and Patsy grabbed at them saying, "Whose are those?"

'I was startled and stumbled back. The gun went off.

'She crumpled over. I saw the blood coming from her head. I did not go to her assistance. I could not face reality. I just thought of the tragedy with my brother.'

He sobbed as he went on: 'I didn't believe it could happen to me a second time.'

He said: 'It was just like seeing a television screen coming up all over again.'

So instead of going for help he panicked and faked the robbery.

Did you, asked the barrister defending him, Mr John

Matthew QC, pull the trigger to murder her? 'I didn't, I didn't, Oh Christ,' Wilfred pleaded.

He said: 'I loved my wife, to kill her was the last thing I wanted to happen.'

He shook with emotion as he said, 'My wife Patsy was a marvellous woman, effervescent, volatile and tremendous fun. She had a great zest for life.'

He admitted he had been Carol's lover for six years and his wife and children had found out about the relationship but with the help of lies and friends he managed to persuade his family that the affair was over.

But he was not going to leave his wife for the mistress.

The jury did not believe him. They found him guilty of murder and he looked shaken as they returned their verdict. He continued to shake as Mr Justice Jupp told him:

'This was clearly murder although no doubt one done during the course of a quarrel rather than planned.'

Shocked and shattered he went to the cells to start the mandatory life sentence.

8

Langan

The Hell-Raiser Who Went up in Flames

There are few hell-raisers left, real hell-raisers like Errol Flynn, Trevor Howard, Richard Harris, Peter O'Toole in their younger days, Brendan Behan and Dylan Thomas who were appalling but lovable when in their almighty cups. Peter Langan was one of the survivors, one of the great ones who could attract the high and the mighty, Royalty and showbiz, the rich and the very rich, the superstars and the TV personalities to his restaurant not just for the food but for his antics.

They were legend in the sixties and seventies. His drinking was enormous, starting the day with great gulps of iced cider by the pint just to exercise the liver after the bash of the night before. Then he would turn to Krug which he kept drinking as if it was water – and he loathed water in any form – until the very early hours. At 4 or 5 a.m. he might crash out in his favourite Chinese restaurant or wander back to collapse in his Harley Street flat or, if his long-suffering wife Susan (and they were married for eighteen years) was around, he might make the effort to get back to Essex and Coggeshall; he had to find friendly transport because he never drove on account of his prodigious drinking. He claimed to drink an average of six bottles of champagne a day although some of his friends reckoned that he could get through a dozen or so on a good day.

In his restaurants he would insult the guests which they loved in the same way that people pack the front rows to see certain entertainers, knowing that by sitting there they will get the required stick. He loved to grope and fondle in a friendly way and enjoyed even more daring young ladies to strip in return for limitless drink for the rest of the evening. In Langan's Brasserie which he owned with superstar Michael Caine and wonder-chef Richard Shepherd in the West End he found takers for his outrageous challenge.

He was known to growl like a dog and crawl on all fours to nip at diners' legs and ankles like a dog. In fact on one occasion he created the newspaperman's favourite headline of 'Man bites Dog' by taking a chunk out of a dog that was annoying customers.

There were many stories about him, some true, some apocryphal. He was said to have smashed a piano because he did not like what the pianist was playing and crashed onto a table where Princess Margaret was sitting because he wanted somewhere to rest his head.

One story he did not deny was being called to the ladies' room by a woman customer who claimed she had found a cockroach and pointed to it. Peter took one look and said, 'Madam, that cockroach is dead. All ours are alive,' and promptly ate it, washed down inevitably with champagne.

One story he did deny was that he was sick into a napkin in front of a young lady journalist who had been sent to interview him. Peter was always good copy because of his abusive and sometimes obscene language to those whom – for no apparent reason – he found objectionable. News editors knew they would always get good quotes from Peter. But on this occasion he was accused of being sick. He strenuously denied this, saying that a piece of food had become stuck in his throat and that he would never vomit in front of a lady because he was very particular about his manners.

Whatever he claimed about his manners his lifestyle was such that he was a character in a decade when there were few characters about.

He was born in 1941, the son of a former Irish rugby full-back and oil chief, Dan, and worked in oil and as a petrol-pump attendant before becoming a restaurateur and starting Odin's in Devonshire Street, Marylebone, in 1966. His self-taught cooking, which was excellent, and his passion for pictures and his ever-increasing idiosyncrasies combined to make it a favourite for up and coming young artists who are now the top names in modern art: Proktor, Bacon, Kitaj, Lucian Freud and Hockney. Like the old French restaurants he would exchange a meal for a painting.

He opened Langan's Brasserie in 1976 with Caine and Shepherd. It was an immediate success and Peter made it. He would wander among the tables chatting to the likes of Prince Andrew, Princess Michael of Kent, Dudley Moore – he insulted him majestically and very rudely – Mick Jagger, Richard Harris, Billy Connolly, Pamela Stephenson, Joan Collins, Roger Moore, Liz Taylor, Johnny Carson, Marlon Brando, John McEnroe and many, many more, a casting list that would delight any agent. Around 600 covers went through a day, customers spending a lot or a little however the fancy took them as it was run as a French restaurant, ordering what one liked.

Peter was the cabaret, all seventeen stone of him; he carried on until sleep finally took over and he would crash out where he was, on the floor, on a table or a chair, upside down or on his back, lying there like a great white whale in his crumpled white suit and staying there until he woke to start again.

He would boast, 'I am a great restaurateur' and then add 'but as a businessman ...' and spread his arms expressively and nod at his friend, Richard, the master chef. He also said, 'Maybe I am a chancer. Time will tell if I am a bum.'

But the life he led, the drinks he swallowed, his behaviour towards his wife and his colleagues began to accumulate. There was another side, a soft gentle man who loved art and poetry, but the public did not see that. It was his troubles that they began to hear and read about.

First his venture into the American restaurant world did not go well. He lost money and claimed that Michael Caine would not back him.

It started going public when Peter, having consumed even more than usual, removed Caine's special table in the window of the restaurant. When he realized a few days later the impact of this he put the table back – but the actor did not return. He said that he did not like Peter because he was a drunk and he did not like drunks. He said he had made a lot of money as a partner but had had no fun so he was quitting.

Peter lurched back. He struck viciously declaring: 'He's very second rate really, as boring as yesterday. He's a mediocrity and the trouble with Michael is that he has a council-house mind.'

It was rude but Caine was just as unpleasant in return. He said: 'You would have a more interesting conversation with a cabbage than with Langan because he is a 24-hour-a-day drunk.'

Caine never went back and Peter spent less time at the restaurant. He was trying to write his autobiography and go on the wagon. Much worse was that he and his wife were not getting on. He had opened a restaurant in Coggeshall which was popular and in the spring of 1988 he and his wife moved into a beautiful cottage in Alphamstone about ten miles from Coggeshall. Alphamstone is a hamlet of about 160 people and they all knew Peter and his reputation but in the quiet of the Essex countryside he was always perfectly well behaved in public.

But he and his wife were rowing in private and in October she went on holiday with a girlfriend to Florence and when she came back she, as owner of the cottage, took proceedings to get the no-longer-lovable Irish drunk out.

In the early hours of 21 October neighbours, police and fire brigade were called to the cottage which was burning fiercely to destruction.

Susan had jumped ten feet from a window and Peter was in a terrible state, having apparently set fire to himself and then been blown out of the bedroom onto the lawn by the force of the petrol explosion.

His old friend Richard Shepherd said: 'It was a pure accident.'

What Susan saw in the daylight was devastation. The roof had caved in and the top floor was gutted and the bottom in not much better condition. Peter did not see it and never was to. He was taken to the burns unit in

Billericay and lingered there, very ill, unable to talk and most of the time unconscious.

Police made inquiries and discovered the couple had had 'a savage domestic row'.

Peter underwent two skin-grafting operations but he was on a ventilator and caught jaundice. Across the Atlantic his shocked partner Michael Caine said he would fly home to see Peter once he was well enough to have visitors. Their silly quarrel, he said, had been patched up and was never really very much.

He said: 'I knew Peter had his troubles, we all did. But I never knew things had gone as bad as this. The trouble with Peter has always been drink. We all tried to get him off it, but it never worked. But he never gave any indication that he would harm anyone or take his own life. He did himself enough damage with drink.'

Police waited patiently for Peter to recover so they could interview him. A file on what had happened that night and a statement from Susan were sent to the Crown Prosecution Service to see if criminal proceedings should be taken against him.

Peter, who had terrible first-degree burns, got no better despite everything the medical staff did. Life went on as always in the Brasserie in Piccadilly but it was all over for the man who made it.

He died on 7 December, taking what was in his mind the night the fire destroyed him and his home with him.

There was an inquest six weeks later, on 20 January 1989. It was held at Brentwood by the very experienced coroner Dr Charles Clark, whose career spanned several terrible Essex occasions like the Saffron Walden Rose and Crown Hotel fire in the early hours of Boxing Day (1969) when eleven died and more would have done so but for one couple not going straight to sleep and smelling smoke and raising the alarm.

His widow Susan, forty-seven, was there and for the first time the whole story was told of what happened that terrible night in their £250,000 home in Alphamstone, just in Essex with the Suffolk border a stride down the road. It was a story so typically Peter, the grand gesture, the hell-raiser turning fire-raiser and going out in a bizarre but quite awful blaze. It collected the headlines that he was used to all his life but this time it was too late for him to see them, to read the sorry end that fate brought him as he lost everything.

First the drama of what happened on the night of 20 October was outlined by the officer in the case, Detective Inspector David Delamain. He said that he had pieced it together from many inquiries but it had to be borne in mind that Peter had never regained consciousness and had never had a chance to challenge what was said about him.

The couple, he said, had been married for eighteen years. In public Peter had behaved in a manner that was 'totally outrageous and well chronicled.

'As time went on Susan Langan who is a quiet, well-mannered likeable person found his behaviour in public unacceptable. Over the years she had more and more faded away from the social scene.'

The coroner listened quietly. It was well known, said the inspector, 'that Peter Langan spent many days away from home on a binge, turning up in a taxi, usually in the morning.'

In October Susan took a short Italian holiday in Florence with a friend and when she returned on 7 October Peter was not at home. The inspector went on, as the press pens sped across the pages recording every word:

'She soon discovered he was at the brasserie drinking heavily. When he arrived home he almost immediately challenged his wife about whether she had a lover and she admitted she had.'

He ordered her out.

Soon after Susan, who had a 50-year-old bachelor boyfriend who worked for the BBC, left the house and three days later contacted solicitors. The following day she obtained a High Court order to allow herself back into her house and a few more days later she obtained another order, this time to evict Peter, which was issued on 18 October.

That same day Susan went home and Peter was sober and welcomed her; she found that the house was nice and tidy. He took her out to dinner and they talked and when they came home they talked more late into the night and slept in separate bedrooms.

But, the inspector went on, when Peter found out that she was trying to evict him he became very angry and there was a row but eventually after Susan agreed to delay the order he was apparently placated. They had a drink and went out to dinner in a restaurant in Colchester.

They drank a bottle of champagne and one of wine between them before returning home just before midnight and they talked long into the night again about their future over another bottle of wine until nearly three o'clock. Everything was relaxed, so relaxed that they took the dog, Peter's dog Megan, a collie cross, out for a walk after midnight.

Then they went to bed and the first real shocking revelation of the inquest came out. The inspector said that they agreed to sleep together as it was likely to be their last night together before separation.

Peter took three sleeping tablets and a tranquillizer. He locked the door and asked Susan to get undressed which she thought was a normal 'preamble to making love' and did as she was requested.

After getting undressed, the inspector said, Peter told her to look into the walk-in wardrobe in the bedroom. Inside was a yellow plastic bag and from it Peter took out a bottle. It was a bottle of petrol and she was in a trap.

Peter began to shake the bottle and then he put it under his arm and took another bottle out of the bag and took out a box of matches which he started to wave around. By this time Peter was staggering around, the inspector said, as if he was feeling the effects of drinks and drugs, this great heap of a man who had drunk enough to launch a hundred thousand ships, and Susan was terrified.

So terrified, that naked she raced through the bedroom and leapt from a balcony in complete darkness to fall fifteen feet through the night and crash to the ground, breaking her heel. She fell on a pathway and managed to drag herself screaming to a neighbour's house.

Fifteen minutes later the neighbours heard a muffled explosion from the Langans' house and flames could be seen.

What on earth had Peter been doing during those fifteen minutes? What had he been thinking about, what had he in mind? The inspector was in no doubt. He said:

'The evidence indicates that he had undergone considerable preparation by preparing the petrol and matches in a bag before confronting his wife.

'It was a trap. She was obviously in fear of her life. She was so terrified that she had to make her escape.

'There are a considerable number of questions as to Peter Langan's actions that night. It would appear he set a trap for his wife either intending to kill her or himself or setting fire to the house.'

He gave his verdict of the behaviour. Inspector Delamain said:

'He intended to do it in the manner of the grand exhibition which would fit in with his character.'

But he added his rider. 'It is fair to say we were never in the position to know what was going on in his mind.'

Did his wife? Fair-haired Susan, wearing a black turban-style bonnet and carrying a black shawl over a dark jumper and checked skirt, gave her evidence as best she could, occasionally shaking at the terror of the night and for her lost husband.

She told of the last dinner, an evening which was 'agreeable and happy' which ended when he asked her to sleep with him just once more before she went ahead with her divorce action. As they had got on as well as they had done together for years she agreed.

She undressed and lay on the bed and then her husband produced the petrol. And he had the matches in his hand.

She said, remembering a bad, bad dream:

'He shook the bottles at me with the caps on. For the life of me I cannot remember what he said.'

But, she said, she was in fear of her life.

'I was panic-stricken. I was terrified of being burnt.'

Did he appear angry, the coroner asked in his quiet unemotional voice? No, said Susan, he appeared very controlled. She explained that he was not entirely steady on his feet and his speech was slurred as he waved about the two Malvern water bottles he had filled with petrol.

But she said, 'Peter was used to making grand gestures

and threats to blackmail me into getting his own way. He was very volatile.'

It was the view of a wife who had become embarrassed by her husband's behaviour in public and knew all his tricks at home.

She said that in her terror she jumped. She landed heavily, and then ...

'I heard Peter call very low in a reasonable sort of voice "Susan, Susan". He just called me twice.

'I did not answer. I was frightened that he would throw the bottle of petrol after me.'

She wished she had for she said: 'I feel now that if I had answered all this might have been avoided.'

And when the coroner said that it was hard for him to resist the conclusion that Peter had intended to take his own life she disagreed.

No, she explained, 'I think he just sort of lost control and wanted to make a great gesture, something to show me despair and feelings of misery that the marriage should come to an end.'

'And of losing you?' the coroner questioned further.

'Yes, losing me.'

'If I said he took his life you would not agree?'

'I find it hard to accept,' his widow said. 'He was so very careful not to lose it in other ways.' It was a fair answer as all his friends knew.

That was not the end of the questioning. Her counsel, Michael Kallipetis, also asked a few to show Peter's state of mind.

Susan said that before the fire they had been discussing how they would divide their property. Was Peter, asked the barrister, showing any signs at all of being desperate or not intending to fulfil their plans?

'No, absolutely not,' Susan replied firmly.

She went on to explain: 'The business really concluded with the thought that after a few years we might get back together again and remarry.

'I think he was devoted to me and indeed he depended on me.'

Then sadly she told of the last words her husband ever spoke to her.

As he was being put into the ambulance he said to her: 'Susan, it was meant for me.' His last words to her as he was inside the ambulance, their wonderful house a burning wreck in the background, the fire lighting the sky, were:

'Susan, are you staying?'

When she was further questioned she still insisted that she did not believe Peter had intended to take his life. She said quietly:

'I have never believed that he would do anything of the kind.

'He has threatened me once or twice when in a high emotional state or perhaps debilitated by his excessive habits but I have never believed that he would. He has always been a man who is extremely careful to avoid such risks.'

She admitted that in the past he had used emotional blackmail to persuade her to agree to things she did not want to do. But not this.

There were other witnesses to try to help fill the fifteen-minute gap after Peter had begun to threaten his wife with the petrol and then had appeared burning in the garden. Had he been blown out of the window by the force of the explosion he had created? Was the explosion deliberate or an accident, a grand gesture or a final despairing act because he knew he had lost the woman he loved?

Next-door neighbour Francis Ranger said he was woken about a quarter to four in the morning by Susan screaming for help. He went outside and found Susan.

And then he heard Peter calling 'Susan, Susan' and his voice appeared to be 'perfectly reasonable'.

Mr Ranger said it was obvious that Susan was terrified because she wanted him to bolt the door of his house and call the police. He did so and about fifteen minutes later he heard the sound of crackling coming from the Langans' house. It was on fire.

Then he saw Peter sitting on a seat in the garden with his back to the wall and at first he did not see any sign of burns. Peter was muttering almost to himself but Mr Ranger heard him say:

'It is only a normal domestic disturbance that has got out of hand.'

It was an understatement.

When police constable Barrie Schultz arrived in the garden Peter called to him.

'I'm over here,' he said. 'It's me you are looking for, my wife is out. I did it, you know, I set the house on fire with petrol.'

But then Peter seemed to contradict himself. He said:

'I wanted to die but I didn't want her to die. I did it. I started the fire with matches and petrol. The petrol was in milk bottles.

'I just wanted to end it all. We were going to die, we were going to die. Can you get done for damaging your own house?'

That was not all Peter told the policeman. He said that he had not slept for four days. That fitted in with what Susan told the coroner:

'Peter was a man given to self-dramatizing, very volatile in temperament. He was rather given to trying to make his fantasies real. In the preceding three days he had a bit of time alone at the house, I think setting up this kind of thing would be fulfilling a fantasy and a way of containing the misery in which he found himself.'

The coroner then gave his verdict. He said that having heard from Susan that her husband did not intend to commit suicide but make a grand gesture to try to dissuade her from leaving him he recorded an open verdict.

That was the end of the official business. But a few days later Susan spoke publicly about it. She talked of how she missed him, how she was convinced that it was not trying to commit suicide.

She said: 'There's not even a tiny possibility that that was his intention. He was deeply upset because I had asked for a divorce. He just meant to frighten me and to demonstrate how deeply he felt for me.'

She gave her own answer to why he drank, not based on emotional nor business problems. 'This self-destructive nature is so often found in the Irish. I don't think people realized how depressed he got.

'He would get very melancholy when his friends weren't around and continue drinking on his own or with people he just picked up.

'Peter was best when he was creating a new restaurant but couldn't cope when it was up and running. That's when he became his drunken worst.'

She was still shocked by the realization that the fire would kill him as well as destroy her home. She never thought of it.

'When we were carted off in the ambulance I had no idea how serious it was, and nor did Peter. He was still conscious and talking all the way to Colchester.

'Of course he had terrible burns on his body but I had every expectation that he would get over it and soon be out of hospital.

'Then it suddenly dawned on me when he was lying unconscious on a life-support machine that it was much more serious.'

He was, it was. What she missed most now that he was gone, she said, was the generous side of her husband, the witty, warm-hearted extrovert that his drinking sometimes hid.

'He was a deeply sensitive man who cared what his friends thought. He was very fond of writing poems, often about love, and would leave them lying about for me to find.'

He had hoped to go and live in Cornwall to write and paint and open a restaurant. Instead his ashes were scattered near his birthplace in County Clare.

And as with everything in the Triangle there was one more mystery. His dog Megan was in the bedroom and was later found limping in the road, blown out of the window too, Susan surmised.

9

Diane Jones

Vanished on the Doorstep

Nothing is so awful as someone disappearing never to be found again. In Norfolk it has happened several times. April Fabb went on her cycle to deliver her sister's birthday present at a village near Cromer. She was thirteen, Norfolk rosy-cheeked with blonde hair and as pretty as any picture. Six minutes after she left home her cycle was spotted in a field. No one has ever seen April since the moment she left home – just six minutes, a miserable six minutes, time to run a mile and a bit – to this day. That happened in 1964.

In the same year a boy of eleven in a town some twenty miles inland went off to see the circus on a Bank Holiday. He never came home and has never been seen nor heard of again. Just what happened in both cases can only be supposition.

Both happened in such a short space of time. One moment they were there, the next they were gone and gone forever, causing immense distress to their parents. In both cases the parents have never stopped grieving.

Nearly as bad is when a person disappears in a short space of time and then is found but not until a long time has passed.

Such was the case with Diane Jones, wife of a Coggeshall doctor. One moment she was by their car in the drive of their luxury house, the next she was gone, not to be seen alive again by her husband but found dead three months later twenty-five miles away in Suffolk, her head battered in with a slater or tiler's hammer. It was a killing that added to the myth of Coggeshall, that it was the village of the Damned.

But who killed her and where she went and how she went remains a mystery to this time of writing in 1990. It was 25 July 1983 when Diane, aged thirty-five and two months pregnant, flounced away from her husband Dr Robert Jones, forty-one, in the drive of their home, Lees Farm, wearing a flowing Indian-style mauve summer dress and high-heeled sandals. By the time he had opened the house and taken her poodle in and gone back for her not more than six minutes had passed.

She was not to be seen nor to be found until October.

But first, the background. She came from Tealby, Lincolnshire, a quiet village where she grew up happily, the only child of a builder and his head teacher wife. She had a winning, flashing smile but was a bit difficult and when she left school she had refused to sit her exams and did not know what she wanted to do. She settled for hairdressing and at the age of sixteen took a two-year course in Lincoln and then worked in salons in Sheffield and Grimsby before her father set her up in her own business which she ran successfully from home. She was very popular and people came from other villages to let her do their hair.

But she was restless, a trait that followed her through her short life, and after two years as a good and busy village hairdresser she gave it all up and went to college to take O and A levels. She passed these and then fell in love and married.

Her husband owned a pig farm in a neighbouring town and after a whirlwind romance they married and she settled down. After a time they moved south to Essex where her husband managed a farm and she decided she would like to become a social worker. She went back to college again to study for the right qualifications.

Their marriage, however, began to crumble and in 1977 she met the second man in her life, a swimming pool official called Paul and she moved in with him in Coggeshall. She also started work as a social worker in nearby Braintree and all seemed well.

But in 1978, a year later, her life changed dramatically when her mother died.

Diane was terribly upset and to help herself face the fact and the world, she began to drink and then drink more and more. Her relationship with Paul began to deteriorate and there were rows and eventually Diane tried to kill herself.

The small town's GP was called in to try to cure her. He was Dr Robert Jones, like Diane a person with one broken marriage behind him. He was married at that time to a woman called Sue and had been for eleven years.

But the doctor and the social worker quickly found a mutual attraction and soon became lovers. Within a short time his wife had moved out and in 1981 Diane left Paul and moved in with the doctor. There were rows and disagreements but whatever happened the doctor and Diane got back together.

Paul was not aware of the romance to begin with and only realized what was going on when Diane went out of the house and off for a three-week cycling holiday in France with her new man.

Eventually in 1982 the relationship with Jones became so tempestuous that she moved into lodgings in Tolleshunt Major where she stayed for just a month before – to the astonishment of former social-worker colleagues – she moved out again and married Dr Jones.

It was not long before Diane moved out again and started taking lovers and drinking. It was around that time that she appeared in court on a drink–driving charge having driven down the A12 dual carriageway the wrong way because, her solicitor said, of the emotional strain of her bizarre relationship with the doctor.

It was not always unhappy. There were candlelight dinners, wonderful nights of love, exciting foreign holidays, even the baby that she longed for. But she could not cope and eventually the baby had to be taken into care. She told Paul whom she still saw that her life had been blown to pieces, that it no longer had any meaning.

And she started to really drink. She was a wild woman, stopping cars and lorries, asking the astonished drivers to make love to her. Just how many different men she had sex with, just how many lovers she had no one will ever know but the police were amazed when they came to probe her lifestyle, which inevitably was the talk of Coggeshall. While her husband went on his rounds so she went on hers, a path leading to disaster.

In the early summer of 1983 she and her husband went on holiday to the south of France. Her drinking seemed to be more under control but she knew that really her marriage was almost over. She was two months pregnant and fearful that this baby too might be taken away from her.

On 22 July she went to see her solicitor to talk about divorce. Her husband did not know this and it came out later that when she vanished he did not immediately report her missing for two reasons: that he believed that she was going to see the solicitor on the Monday after their dinner date and that he might have advised her to take some form of action which meant that she went away. Or he thought that she had just gone away as she had done in the past.

Whatever the rights or wrongs and Dr Jones is emphatic, she was invited to dinner by her husband on the Saturday night and she went and had her hair done in the village hairdresser's and made herself look very desirable for the special meal her husband was going to cook for her in the sixteenth-century farmhouse. There was nothing unusual about such an evening in their strange relationship that fluctuated between passion and misery.

Diane drank and drank and at the end of the meal demanded that her husband take her out which he did, taking her to the Woolpack, an oak-beamed ancient pub about a mile from the house. There they had a drink at the bar, sitting on stools and everything went well until it came to closing time and Dr Jones said it was time to go.

Diane refused so he went to the car with her little dog and came back for her and when she still refused he picked her up bodily, put her over his shoulder and carried her out into the night.

She was in a bad mood and made sure he knew that. She was moaning in the car and made him stop halfway along the drive of their house because she did not want to be with him and she might have left her handbag in the pub and she wanted to be out of Coggeshall and to escape from him.

Her husband left her to give the dog a final run before going into the house. He reckons the time gap was about five or six minutes. When he went into the house he expected to see her lying on the sofa or having a drink.

She was not there and he did not see her alive again.

He reported her missing nine days later and from the start the police suspected him.

It did not help that he had sold his Peugeot, the car in which he had driven Diane home, a few days after she vanished and when police saw the new owner, it had been steam-cleaned and any clues, should there have ever been any clues, had gone. Dr Jones was quite open about it. He said that it had been advertised for sale before his wife, who often went missing for days, had disappeared. He was open about everything, particularly in his insistence that he had not killed his wife and had absolutely no idea where she was.

The police interviewed him time after time. He never wavered. They took dogs into the area and large numbers of men and searched and searched and found nothing. They put frogmen into a nearby reservoir and found nothing. They made house-to-house inquiries which produced nothing. They interviewed lovers, many of whom were most anxious that neither their wives nor anyone else should find out and that produced nothing either. They interviewed Paul and Dr Jones's second wife, who was most supportive to her ex-husband, but they could not help either.

Dr Jones picked up the pieces of his life even though the floorboards of his house had been ripped up, the chimneys inspected, the roadside verges dug up.

The police also discovered that Diane had predicted that she would disappear at a New Year's Eve party. She was not saying that her husband would have anything to do with it but more than she would arrange her disappearance, her friends told the police. One friend told the police that from her behaviour it was clear that she was mentally disturbed and emotionally depressed.

Then another friend came forward to give another

version of Diane's predictions for the future. She had told this friend that she feared that she would be killed and that her killer would get rid of her in such a way that she would never be found. That forecast was just a month before she married Dr Jones and she had kept a diary up to that time when staying with the woman friend.

But Diane's prediction only partly came true. In the bizarre way that she lived, so she died and after three long months she was found.

A beater out on an autumn shoot found her body in undergrowth at Brightwell over the border in Suffolk. She was still wearing the Indian-style dress and a post-mortem showed that she had died within a few hours of leaving her husband by his car. Some of her teeth were missing and she had been beaten with a hammer so terribly that she was practically unrecognizable.

Brightwell is over thirty miles from Coggeshall. It is an easy drive, down the A12, round Ipswich on the A45 loop and then back onto the A12. If Diane had walked in her drunken fashion to the main A120 Braintree to Colchester road, which joins the A12 before the garrison town, had hitched a lift and found a kindred spirit who had had a drink too many, who had an overwhelming desire, had been thwarted in his lust off the main road by a woman who could switch and change like a chameleon and then in his rage had beaten her to death with a tiler-type hammer, there could be an answer to the question of who killed her.

But from then until now there has been no answer. The police moved heaven and earth to try to find one and the person they were sure could provide it was Dr Jones.

He knew it and as they removed furniture from his home, took off his newly painted seven-bar gate he declared vehemently:

'The finger of suspicion is pointing at me. There is no one else for the police to point it at.'

They had him in for fifty-five hours, fifty-five long hours during which he was grilled. All he could do was to repeat what he had said all along: that she got out of the car and wanted to go back for her bag and that was the last he ever saw of her.

Yes it was true that her jewellery and her watch were not there but he did not know where they were. No, he did not want her removed, no, he had not killed her, no, he did not know where she had gone nor why and he had certainly not murdered her. At last the police let him go but on bail which meant that he had to report to the police station from time to time. Because the police were still pretty sure it was him and as he said on television, he was tempted to accept their offer to confess so that they would make sure he did not spend too long in prison; but only for a moment, because he knew that he had nothing to do with his wife's murder.

The police collected all the statements, all the forensic evidence, all the information they had and sent it to the Director of Public Prosecutions to see if he thought there was enough to make a jury convict a person who was charged.

From February until April the Director's office studied the fat file and finally came to the conclusion that there was insufficient evidence to take any action. The police statement made it crystal clear how the land lay. It said:

'The Suffolk Constabulary has been advised by the Director of Public Prosecutions that, as matters stand, there is insufficient evidence to justify the institution of proceedings against Dr Jones for the murder of his wife. Inquiries into the death of Diane Jones will continue.'

The DPP's office would not add to the statement. Dr Jones went along to the police station to hear the verdict rather as he would to his surgery and afterwards he said:

'No one in my position could fail to be relieved that the constant pressure of the past nine months will be lifted. I have had to put up with the continuous attentions of the media, with people parked outside my house day and night and cameras trained on my windows.'

The news was given to him by Detective Chief Superintendent Eric Shields, then head of Suffolk CID, and then the doctor's solicitor added a few words. He said:

'Dr Jones has maintained his innocence throughout and this conclusion is entirely consistent with that. Now he just wants to be left alone and lead his life in peace.'

That was hoping for a lot because the media and thus the people of Britain and abroad were still interested in Dr Jones and when the killer of his wife would be found. He found other lady friends and went on living in the house – until he sold it – to which the police returned everything they had taken away including his gate. The police had dug up his garden seven times in the course of their inquiries and found nothing. They had excavated a trench by the side of the town's bypass and found nothing.

Now Dr Jones was a free man with suspicion lifted and they had to look elsewhere. But where? There was no evidence against the doctor and there were no clues to lead them to anyone else, to none of the many men in her life.

The clearing of Dr Jones meant that at last there could be an inquest and that Diane could be buried.

At the inquest in Ipswich on 20 April 1984 there was little fresh to record. The pathologist, Professor Geoffrey Austin, said that she had died from four skull fractures caused by a blow to the head. There was no evidence that she had been strangled.

The coroner recorded a verdict that she had been unlawfully killed which everyone knew and released her body for burial. She was buried next to her mother in her home village in Lincolnshire.

Afterwards Detective Chief Superintendent Shields said that the murder inquiry would continue. Four years on it is still running but has gone no further.

For Diane's is one of three unsolved murders in Suffolk, all being cases of bodies being dumped in the county, not killed there. Two are from the Triangle, poor Linda Smith who still clutched the ten-shilling note her grandmother had given her to go and buy a paper but who was snatched from the street as she looked in the newsagent's shop window, and Diane Jones, who may well have volunteered to go on the ride that ended in her brutal murder for a reason only the killer knows and is unlikely to tell now unless his conscience makes him.

The third was a London boy aged sixteen who went missing and ended up in a suitcase in eight pieces behind a hedge just outside Ipswich on the A12. He had been strangled and the killer had taken the gruesome and macabre step of cutting up his body into pieces. When the case was found – and Chief Superintendent Shields was on the inquiry as a detective inspector – it was obvious that whoever had done such a terrible crime was also an expert in surgery, whether it be human or animal.

The boy was identified in a bizarre way too. There was no indication as to who he was or where he came from and he fitted no description of anyone missing anywhere in Britain. So the police asked one of the very experienced press photographers there from London – and in those days all of Fleet Street turned out to join the local press on murder investigations like this because they were big news – to help.

With a police photographer and a surgeon they were able to photograph the head without making it appear anything other than the head of a living boy and it was published all over the country.

His father had the horrific shock of seeing his son's face peering out from the front page of the now defunct *Evening News* in London and had the even more appalling task of going down to Suffolk to identify him.

But although they then knew who he was and where he was from and who his friends were the police never found his killer, although they did have strong suspicions of one man who had the necessary skills and pattern of sexual behaviour and came from the same area as the boy, but he died.

It is not altogether surprising that the boy's body was dumped there. The ease with which criminals move round the country, robbing and vanishing up the motorway system is part of modern life. There is no reason why bodies should not be left in the same way. It has happened up and down the M1/M6 and other motorways. And there is no doubt that the boy's body was left where it was because the killer wanted to be rid of it.

It is true that Linda was also dumped but that was almost certainly by someone who knew the area and was a local man or a former local man visiting.

In the case of poor alcohol-soaked, sex-mad Diane Jones, she may well have been killed at the spot where she was found, either in the car or somewhere near where she lay – and the gap before finding her was so long that any blood or similar clues would have long been washed away – and the killer walked away and left her.

Perhaps one day we will know who he was; who the man who murdered Linda was or is. Perhaps one day he will be so haunted by what he has done, by his victim's face at the moment he struck, that he will admit it.

Or maybe not.

10

Hailstone

Killed for a Drink

Colchester taxi driver Henry Hailstone died as the European leaders planned to cry havoc and unleash the dogs of war against the Nazis in Occupied Europe. Until the day arrived when they would cross the Channel the dogs remained kennelled and bored all over the south of England. The idea for D-Day was early summer, some time around June, but the exact date was flexible and depended on various factors. For the young men who waited the sooner it came the better for many were from overseas, particularly north America, and to be in England in winter was an experience that many of them did not like. They were spread in camps from the tip of Kent, in Essex, the eastern counties and right across Surrey, Sussex, the coast of Hampshire, down through Dorset to Devon and Plymouth, all likely areas or gathering points from where the troops would eventually head across the Channel.

Those who waited were often out of their own country, even state, even home town for the first time in their lives. They were in a foreign country and worse, one where it was cold and the people, although speaking the same language, were alien. In Essex the wind blew and in the Triangle it blew extra strong in December, 1943, not because there was anything special about it, but because it always did. It came whistling cold and mean from the Ural Mountains, across the North Sea without a hillock to flatten it and across East Anglia, a wind that went straight through you, lazy and bitter.

For those waiting in the five huge American Army

camps at Birch, just outside Colchester, there was little to do except be attracted to the bright lights of London, the clubs that glittered behind the black-out screens, to the pubs that had drink for the bored young men who wanted to pass time, and girls and women who were ready for sex at any time. They, like the men, did not expect to have a long life; there were always the German bombs for the girls, the bullets for the men.

Henry Hailstone, who was twenty-eight, a bachelor and a big heavy man, came into the story as a victim of the dogs of war because of the London factor. He lived in lodgings in Colchester, was known as a pleasant young man who was careful with his money and was competent at his job despite having bad hands due to an accident some years before.

Just after eleven in the evening of Tuesday 7 December 1943, he called in at his lodgings in Maldon Road to tell his landlady that he would be late for supper because he had to take two GIs back to the camp at Birch five miles away.

He did not come back for his supper.

The next day the taxi, a Vauxhall belonging to a Colchester firm, was found in Haynes Green Lane in a village near Clacton-on-Sea some miles from Colchester. The local bobby out on his bike had spotted it and had a look inside. There lying on the seat were a man's jacket and a blood-stained mac. He went to tell his sergeant who went to have a look and called in the top Essex CID man who, in those days, was George Totterdell. He and his inspector drove out to Copford and had a look at the clothes.

It was clear that the jacket had been pulled off its owner from the back and the mac – equally new – had bloodstains around the back collar. In the pockets they found various articles including the driver's licence.

After seeing Hailstone's landlady they went to have a look at the taxi. Its windows were closed but the lights and brakes were on, the ignition turned off.

Inside there were signs of a struggle. All the driver's papers were scattered and the upholstery was scratched. Although there were a couple of sixpenny bits in the taxi, the driver's wallet and his precious Canadian lighter, a mysterious keepsake he took everywhere with him, were gone.

As the two detectives, using a dimmed torch so as not to break black-out regulations, continued their search they found blood spots on the rearside and window.

It looked very much as though the driver had been violently rolled and killed for whatever he had on him – and the detectives knew that would not be much – and then taken somewhere in the back of his cab and dumped.

Because it was wartime and there were few Englishmen around suspicions immediately fell on the Americans in general and the two men, whom Hailstone had said he was driving to the bases, in particular. Police knew they were coloured, one a GI, the other possibly an officer, and that out in the camps were many coloured men.

The US garrison headquarters in Colchester was notified and their police, known as Snowdrops, offered their help at once. They started trying to find who had called a cab to take the men to Birch on 7 December.

At dawn the next day, the British bobbies began to search the area for the body of the missing taxi driver. It was found under a blackberry bush in the grounds of Birch Rectory and it was obvious that his killer had driven him along the road and when he spotted a convenient spot he and his companion, because Hailstone's weight demanded that two men were needed to move him, pushed him under the wire and let him roll. He came to a halt under the bush which broke his roll, the spot not being visible from the main road.

His trouser pockets had been turned inside out and his face was caked in blood. There was no sign of a struggle which confirmed the dumping.

Dr Francis Camps arrived, inspected the body and then carried out a post-mortem which showed that Hailstone had been strangled manually and hit three times as well.

It appeared that the murder had been committed for money, a typical murder of a taxi driver by passengers. There were thousands of Americans and among them were going to be the two rollers. It was just a case of finding them and the first positive lead came from a Canadian captain who had arrived at the camp with a coloured GI two days before the driver went missing. By mistake the American left his gas mask behind (and took the captain's mac with a Rolex wristwatch in the pocket) when they parted.

The name in the gas-mask box was J. Hill, with the number 1031. The Snowdrops quickly discovered the owner of the gas mask who admitted it was his but he had lent it to another GI called George Fowler who was also traced and agreed he had borrowed it to go on leave to London.

The Canadian captain had been traced because his mac had been found six miles further down the Maldon road, lying in a gutter. In one pocket was a new American service emblem, in the other a Canadian maker's label with the words Captain J.J. Weber written in the collar. Canadian Army police traced the captain who said that he had met a coloured US sergeant at Liverpool Street Station in London, had struck up a friendship and when they reached the captain's barracks at Cherry Tree Camp on the outskirts of Colchester he invited him back to his mess for a drink. While he was out of the room the sergeant departed with his mac with five pounds in notes, a Rolex wristwatch, a torch and a pair of gloves in the pockets and a bottle of whisky.

The captain's story was confirmed by the mess orderly who remembered that the black American had left his gas mask behind and it was still there.

The police went to see Private George E. Fowler who told a long, highly unlikely and rambling story about how he had gone on leave to London on 1 December and had caroused and drunk and had fun with friends and women non-stop until 8 December when he arrived back at camp in the middle of the evening wearing a sergeant's uniform. He had absolutely no idea how he came to have the uniform or why he was wearing it. 'Guess I must have been drugged,' he volunteered.

As far as he could recall he had left the gas mask at the Liberty Club. The discrepancies in the statement made the detectives very suspicious and they detained him. While he was in the cells they went to his hut and searched it.

Above his bed was the sergeant's uniform with traces of

blood on it. Inside his kitbag was a pawn ticket from a pawnbroker in Cannon Street in the City of London for a Rolex watch to the value of three pounds and issued to a Charlie Huntly of the 356 Engineers Regiment, the same outfit as Fowler's. It was dated 6 December, the day after Captain Weber had lost his watch while in Fowler's company.

Superintendent Totterdell asked Fowler about this and he said that he had never pawned a watch in his life, he had never had a watch since his arrival in England, and he did not know what a pawnbroker ticket was like. He volunteered to make another statement to cover the whole incident of his good time in London. In this he said that the pawn ticket the police had discovered he had found in the West Indies Club in the West End of London on 3 December. It was three days earlier, the police immediately noticed, than the actual pawning of the watch. The gas mask, Fowler insisted, was not there when he went back for it.

The next step was to find Charlie Huntly who turned out to be another coloured soldier who had met a Private Leatherberry with another coloured American called George. George had given him a Rolex watch and asked him where he could pawn it. He had pawned it with the Cannon Street broker and he handed the sealed envelope, having put his name on the back, over to George.

The police retrieved the watch from the pawnbroker and it belonged to Captain Weber. Back to Private Fowler went Totterdell and his inspector; this time the American changed his story again and – probably through guilty conscience – gave an account very near the truth, police believed.

He now admitted that he did leave London on 5 December, had a drink with the captain but said that the latter had given him his raincoat. Back at camp he met Leatherberry who suggested that they went to London. Fowler explained that he had already overstayed his leave by two days but the other negro persuaded him and they went back to London and went on the town drinking and having sex until the money ran out.

On 7 December they returned to Colchester and

Leatherberry suggested that they took a cab and roll the driver. They got the cab and four miles on the way Fowler asked the driver to stop so he could go to the toilet.

While away from the taxi he heard Leatherberry calling for him and when he reached it he found the two men struggling. Leatherberry asked him to help, telling him sharply, as he said to the police, that 'I was in it just as much as he was.'

He saw the other man punching the driver in the face as he held him with his left hand and then the driver went limp and Leatherberry was hauling him from the front seat into the back. He repeated that they had got to stick together and began going through the dead man's pockets. He saw a cigarette lighter, some papers and a bill in the other soldier's hands. He said they must get rid of the body and they carried it across the road and slid it under wire fencing.

By that time Fowler had given his colleague Captain Weber's raincoat because he said he was cold. Fowler took the wheel and headed for Maldon to catch a train to London but the last one had gone so they went back to camp and left the taxi where it was found.

Later when he made yet another statement, Fowler said that he had seen Leatherberry using the taxi driver's lighter two days after the murder and admitted giving the stolen watch to Huntly to pawn.

Then police saw Leatherberry who confirmed much of what Fowler, whom he knew as Funely, had told the police with one major exception: he said that he knew nothing about the murder and was in London in a club on the night of the murder. He was closely interrogated but he stuck to his story and would not add another word. As one of the detectives said at the time: 'He shut up like a clam and as such he remained.'

However, he was picked out by Fowler as the man who had been with him in London and who had been in the taxi and the man he had assisted in the murder. At the same parade he was picked out by a man and woman from the club, Freddie's House in London's East End, as one of the servicemen who had been in there on 6 December, not 7 December.

As the evidence piled up police found other soldiers who saw Leatherberry in camp in the early hours after the murder in the company of another soldier they could not recognize.

At the same time police tried to find out how much Hailstone had on him when he was murdered. They could never be sure but it was unlikely to have been more than £12 which the two Americans gambled and drank away.

They rolled and killed him for so little.

Just before Christmas the two men were handed over to their CO to be dealt with. Fowler, who said he did not know how much Leatherberry had taken, was charged with murder, robbery and larceny; Leatherberry, who denied ever taking part in any robbery or murder or even being there, denied charges of murder and robbery.

They both appeared before a general court martial in Ipswich Town Hall on 19 January, with both trials running simultaneously.

Fowler put all the blame for the murder on the other man, repeating the facts that he had given in his statement, that he was away from the car when the attack started and that it was Leatherberry who hit and strangled the taxi driver.

He was found guilty and sentenced to life imprisonment and immediately taken into the other court room to give evidence against his fellow-soldier.

Leatherberry, however, insisted that he had been in London at the time of the murder and any scrapings from under his nails which showed that his hands had been steeped with blood were because of a fight or having sex.

The court did not believe him and he was sentenced to death. He was hanged at the military prison in Shepton Mallet in Somerset on 16 May 1944, less than three weeks before D-Day and the invasion to take part in which he had been trained and brought across the Atlantic.

11

Three Pointless Killings

The trouble with bluff Bill Leyland's chickens was that they strayed from the field next to the pub where his wife was licensee in the village of West Bergholt and went on to next-door neighbour John Perkins's garden.

It was not just chickens. Turkeys, ducks and goats made their way across and started eating vegetables and flowers.

Perkins, a small, quiet and nervous former civil servant, was very upset and spoke to Leyland about it. The strays still kept appearing and from time to time Perkins mentioned it but nothing happened until he instructed his solicitor to write to Leyland and tell him it must stop.

It did. Fencing was put up and the animals stayed their side of it and then for eight years the two men lived in harmony but never spoke to each other.

Then in the summer of 1957 three chickens wandered across into Perkins's garden and began to munch his vegetables. They kept coming, regularly, hungry, annoying the small man.

In the following January Mary Kriek was murdered and police and press began to use the pub in the village. Leyland and his wife made them welcome, feeding them fat sandwiches made from tasty chickens.

The car-park was full and the only unhappy person in the area was Perkins who seethed and got short shrift when he mentioned it to Leyland, a bigger man.

On a Saturday in February Perkins saw Leyland across the fence and asked him what he was going to do about the chickens. Leyland said that he was not going to do much and a heated argument started.

It ended when Perkins – to Leyland's utter astonishment – pulled a Webley 0.45 calibre service revolver from his pocket and without warning nor saying a word shot Leyland dead through the heart.

The big man slumped to the ground and Perkins went back into his house and called the police.

He told them quietly, matter of fact: 'Everything went blurred.'

He stood in the dock at Chelmsford Assizes in the summer and pleaded not guilty to murder but guilty to manslaughter on the grounds that the state of his mind at the time reduced his responsibility.

The judge accepted this and heard that Perkins suffered from a 'chronic anxiety state' and sentenced him to life imprisonment.

It was a case of mindless murder, a man taking another man's life for a very small reason. Three straying chickens are not a reason for murder whatever the state of the killer's mind.

Another senseless murder was that of Miss Susan Southgate in 1957, who was eighty-three and lived on her own at Writtle, near Chelmsford; she comes into the Triangle story because police suspected that her killers came from that area.

Miss Susan was very well known in the village for several reasons but mainly because of her six cats, her boyfriend, the nickname she gave the village bobby because he kept such a close eye on her and the money she kept in the Old Mill House from the property she owned and let.

That fact was talked about and the information could easily have been picked up by a stranger having a drink in the local or going into one of the shops.

Neighbours used to worry about her, particularly because she left the doors open for the cats so that they could come in and out. She told them not to worry because her boyfriend was always about.

He was not on the night that thieves broke in. They had at their mercy a little old lady, quite defenceless against tough young men, but instead of making sure that she kept quiet by gentle means they forced her into her favourite armchair and as she was held, terrified, she was tied and trussed with electric flex and gagged with black insulation tape.

They carried her halfway up the stairs and dumped her. Then they started to ransack the house, taking pound notes from the toast rack and silver from the hollow base of a table lamp. It was well known that that was one of her hiding-places. Having taken all they could find they left, leaving the old lady trussed up like a Christmas turkey in the chair.

Why they left her like that, knowing how old she was, how frail and defenceless, no one knows because the thieves have never been found. But what is known is that they had pangs of conscience as they fled from the scene and they eventually stopped the car and dialled 999. The call was picked up at Scotland Yard but some police involved in the inquiry believed that this was part of their plan to avoid detection, that they could have been locals from east of Chelmsford, perhaps Colchester or Braintree, who had heard talk of the treasures and had carried out the robbery and then headed for London to make a call to Scotland Yard and leave a false trail before heading back to Essex. They only had to drive to Romford to make the call.

Whatever the truth they made the call, telling the officer who took it in the control room at Scotland Yard that if they went to Mill Cottage in Writtle they would find the old lady trussed up and would they go and release her?

Unfortunately they did not give the correct address and it took a police patrol car eighty-five minutes to find the right house, the honeysuckle-covered Old Mill House. There on the stairs in her chair was Miss Southgate.

They were far too late. The old lady had been dead some time, suffocated.

It was a totally pointless crime. Like Perkins they could have used force without hurting her but instead they killed her at the end of her useful life for a bit of cash.

They were not nearly as smart as they thought. When police went through the house they found a treasure trove of gold coins, trinkets, silverware and pound notes in trunks and hidey-holes in the ten rooms. The trunks were as secure as they had made her. They were loaded into police vehicles, the sun glistening on the gold that police had found lying loosely in some drawers.

Another equally meaningless act was the murder of Captain Samuel Grundy, a 57-year-old regular army officer, attached to the 18th battalion of the Essex Home Guard in Colchester just after D-Day in 1944.

He had left battalion headquarters soon after seven on the evening of 22 June to go rabbit shooting in the fields nearby, taking his twelve-bore with him. As he walked he came across a young soldier sitting down near the gravel pit where some bombs had been dropped earlier in the evening. Captain Grundy asked the soldier what he was doing with the gun he was nursing. It was a question that cost him his life.

A short time later the soldier, Private Jones of the Somerset Regiment, knocked on the door of a house on the edge of Colchester and asked the owner to phone the police. He would not say why but when the householder did phone the soldier took the phone and said 'Can you send a police car please. It's a case of killing. My name is Private Jones.'

When a detective arrived, Jones told a strange tale. He said he had shot an officer and explained why. He said that he had broken open a locker in his barracks while his platoon was out training and stolen fifteen shillings. Then fear of facing his friends overcame him and he broke out of camp, planning to steal a gun and hold up a civilian and get his clothes.

Having stolen a sten gun and two magazines of ammunition he was walking along when he decided to have a rest. Then an officer in shirt sleeves came up to him and did not accept his answer to his question as to what he was doing with the gun. When Jones told him he was on an exercise the officer did not believe him.

He ordered him to hand over the gun and there was a struggle. It ended with the soldier pumping bullets into the officer.

'I lost my head and shot him. I must have been mad. I threw the sten gun away,' the soldier said in his first statement.

Detective Chief Inspector Totterdell was the man in

charge. He and other officers made their way to the body during a bombing raid overhead in pitch darkness. On the way they accidentally met the doctor also crossing the marshes to reach the body and the small group went on feeling their way and thus making it a hazardous operation because above the fighters were attacking the German bombers who were dropping their loads so they could make faster speed back to base across the Channel.

When they reached the area where the body was they had to wait for dawn before they could start their investigation.

The first thing they noticed was that Captain Grundy put up a violent struggle for his life. But there was no sign of the shotgun and it was not until some time later that it was found over quarter of a mile away. The stock had been broken from the barrel, suggesting the fight the captain had put up as Jones tried to wrench the gun from him. The sten gun was recovered from a stream nearby with one fully loaded magazine and sixteen rounds of loose ammunition.

Totterdell went to see Jones himself. He went over old ground until he reached the point when Captain Grundy asked him where he got the gun. When the captain did not believe him and wanted to look at the gun Jones jumped back and cocked it. The officer then tried to get it off him and in the struggle it had gone off but Grundy had not been hit.

Jones said that scared him and as Grundy turned and ran down the hill the soldier fired a round after him and thought he had hit him because Grundy put his hand to his back as he was running.

So Jones ran after him and caught him and again there was a struggle and again the officer fled with the soldier trying to fire at him. But the magazine jammed so he had to change it for another one and then set off in pursuit again. He caught him by a barbed-wire fence and they fought again. But this time when the officer, who was thirty-five years older, fell backwards the young soldier fired several shots into him.

'I thought he was dead. He should have been,' he said in his statement.

He had fired six bullets into the top half of the officer's body.

So what kind of man was this young soldier who killed like that because, as he said at the assize court, he lost his temper and fired a burst at a range of eight yards as his victim lay on the ground?

His father was a drunkard and his mother died when he was very young. When he left school he moved in with his sister but broke up the furniture with a hatchet and was certified insane; he was allowed out of the mental institution because they felt his insanity was due to his father's treatment and was not permanent.

He had then turned to thieving and warehouse-breaking but after spending a year in Borstal, a secure institution for young teenage offenders who normally had to serve a minimum of two years of tough discipline and training, he was released and joined the army.

When he appeared in the assize court he said he was angry because of the attempt to take the sten gun from him and lost his temper. His counsel stressed in his address to the jury that there was an alternative to the murder charge to which his client had pleaded not guilty, namely that of manslaughter on the grounds that Jones's temper had become so inflamed that it became ungovernable. There was the point that trying to take a soldier's gun from him was a hazardous thing to do.

It took the jury just twenty minutes to find the soldier guilty of manslaughter, not murder. The judge said he could not imagine a worse case of manslaughter and jailed him for fifteen years.

Perhaps the war and the military training and the use of guns added a spur to his evil temper. Perhaps he was insane although he forbade his barrister permission to raise the question of medical evidence at the trial. Who can say?

Perkins was not responsible for his actions. The gang who killed Miss Southgate definitely were. But the result in all three cases was that people died for very little reason and any life snuffed out in such a way is even more of a tragedy than the normal murder done for lust, passion, hatred or robbery.

12

Greville

Noble Suicide

There was much about Maynard Greville that reminded the people around Great Dunmow of his mother's lover, King Edward VII. Not that there was ever any doubt about Maynard's parentage. He was the third son of the fifth Earl of Warwick and his mother was Daisy, Countess of Warwick and mistress of the king. It was just that Maynard as he grew older looked royal and he had a regal bearing about him with his bristling beard and moustache and his manner.

He was in fact an outstanding journalist, first as a young and jovial reporter who kept his friends in laughter in the Press Club and then later as a motoring and country life expert, based in Great Easton just outside Dunmow. Easton was the country retreat of the king. Maynard was born in 1898, twelve years before the king died, and grew up and stayed in the area.

He was known in the country as an energetic and eccentric cyclist, roaring round the lanes on one of his many racing bikes, dressed in a red beret, ancient plus-fours without a necktie, a rip-roaring character, always full of life and talk.

There was another side to him that became worse when his wife died in the late 1950s and that was his drinking. He eventually became an alcoholic and was treated for it. In his cups he would stride into Dunmow in his dressing-gown, this handsome, arresting man demanding drink in local hotels and then staying to talk with the locals as he drank, never aggressive, never an unwanted companion.

In his latter years he became one of the foremost experts

on trees in the country. His interest was aroused during the Second World War by the actions of the Americans when they wanted to build a runway at nearby Wethersfield. To do so they tore down two dozen 500-year-old oaks and that greatly upset him, so much that he never, ever forgot it.

So great was his interest that he began a vast census of every outstanding tree in Britain, a task so great that his friends thought it was impossible until they saw him at work gradually adding to the list in his file. He toured the south of England, noting the details and taking pictures which were kept with the record. He managed to list some in Scotland too as he widened his travels in pursuit of trees.

At the same time he started planting his own arboretum for the years to come.

It was ironic that he should meet his death in one of his own trees, falling from it and dying five days later in hospital at Bishop's Stortford just over the border into Hertfordshire.

It all seemed such a straightforward and tragic accident as he fell out and injured himself on his 800-acre estate at Easton Lodge, Little Easton on 17 February 1960. He had been up a poplar to cut some of the buds with a carving knife and as he did so he accidentally stabbed himself.

When he was rushed to hospital it was found that he had caused a three-inch wound in the stomach. Before he left for hospital he made a phone call, his daily phone call, his regular call for fifteen years to his close friend since 1928, BBC executive Sunday Wilshin who before the war had been a beauty of the stage and screen.

They had been great friends since 1928 and it was not just a friendship between the Earl of Warwick's uncle and a famous beauty but between her and Maynard's wife too until she died in 1957.

Sunday Wilshin said later: 'I was a friend of his wife also – and they were very happily married until her death – and the rest of his family.'

During the phone call after the accident he told her what had happened, how he stabbed himself by mistake, now he was on the way to hospital.

He died five days later and a post-mortem was performed by a Scotland Yard pathologist and an examination of his waistcoat by Dr Lewis Nickolls, the master forensic scientist from the Metropolitan Police laboratory.

What they discovered changed the whole appearance of the death. It became a suspicious death, no longer the accident that Maynard had told Sunday and his GP, Dr John Tasker at Great Dunmow.

An inquest was held at Bishop's Stortford, Hertfordshire, where he had died, on 21 March 1960, and an amazing story unfolded in the customary clinical language of the medical and forensic scientist which saves so much of the emotional upset that could be caused if such evidence were given more vivid expression.

First the GP told how Maynard had rung him on the evening of 17 February to tell him he had pushed a knife into 'his tummy'. The doctor said that he knew that Maynard had been treated for drinking and alcoholism.

Then Dr Nickolls gave his evidence and he said that he had found eight cuts in Maynard's waistcoat which was not at all what the dead man had told Sunday.

There was one large one, Dr Nickolls said, which could have been caused by a carving knife. The others were 'tentative cuts, typical of a self-inflicted wound'. It was his view that that was what had happened.

Then Sunday, who had come down from London, said that Maynard had told her while in hospital that he had fallen while he was getting up a tree with a knife.

It was all very strange, as odd a death as one could find. The coroner thought so too.

He said: 'Although the people who knew Mr Greville are united in the opinion that he never spoke about taking his own life, after hearing the evidence of three doctors I am satisfied that he did kill himself.'

Afterwards, back in her London flat, Sunday said: 'I still cannot believe that Maynard committed suicide. He had such a vital interest in living, exploring to the last inch everything he was interested in.

'He was the warmest, kindest and most generous man I have ever known.

'Every day for the past fifteen years we talked on the telephone. He would ring me or I would phone him. We had a lot to talk about trees or the many subjects we had in common.

'An affair of the heart? Yes, we had a close personal relationship that few people could share or even understand.

'I was also very friendly with his wife and the rest of the family.'

But why should this Man of the Trees want to kill himself? No one could explain. When the funeral was held at Little Easton church before the inquest verdict – and that would not have altered anything – there was a large turn-out of his friends and relatives including his daughter and son-in-law, his sister Lady Marjorie Beckett, representatives of the Royal Forestry Service, the St. John Ambulance Brigade, the Essex County Land Agent and Barclays Bank.

And in *The Times* this tribute was written of him:

The accident which cost Maynard Greville his life at his home at Easton Lodge, has robbed us at much too early an age of a true English eccentric.

From his talented and beautiful mother, the Countess of Warwick, he inherited high intelligence, defiant originality, unbreakable loyalty and a blazing hatred of hypocrisy. If he disliked you, you and everyone else knew it; if he loved you nothing on earth could shake his affection or his friendship.

Whether in the Press Club when he was a hilarious young reporter and later, a motoring and country life correspondent for serious weeklies, or pedalling furiously about the countryside on one of his fleet of racing bicycles, dressed in a red beret, ancient plus-fours and no necktie, he was always alive, controversial and extremely handsome.

In later years he became one of the country's experts on trees and it is an ironic tragedy that he should have met his death by a fall from one of his own trees in the great arboretum he was planting for the years to come and this only two years after the death of his gentle wife Dora.

He will be mourned and remembered with affection by his many friends everywhere and most of all by the quiet people in the Essex villages round Dunmow where he grew up and lived his life, who knew and loved him as one of themselves.

So why did he do it?

Only he could have told us. He chose not to tell anyone, not even his friend Sunday. Perhaps he had a sudden urge to end his life after the death of his wife, over his drinking problem, over something he had not shared with anyone else. Life is full of such mysteries, people acting in a way that not even those closest to them can guess or understand for in the human mind there are secrets that are locked so tight that only the owner knows them, either to use them for his own pleasure or self-disgust or worry or even – perhaps in the case of Maynard Greville – to make death a better alternative. Years later a famous television broadcaster of the time committed suicide because he could no longer stand the fear of 'It', but was unable to explain what 'It' was to his friends who might have been able to help him. 'It' was something that filled his life to such an extent that he could not live with it any longer and death was preferable.

But is such a mystery any more strange than men who can kill – like the murderers of Linda Smith, Mary Kriek, Diane Jones – and carry on living without any clue to anyone that they have done it? How do they sleep at nights or has their memory put an exclusion zone on the thought?

13

Bamber

Massacre for Money

Murder comes in many forms. It is no respector of person, rank, class or sex and age. When a plan to murder is conceived in cold blood instead of the passion of the moment it is even more evil. All types of murder occur for some reason or another: revenge, hatred, robbery, removal of an unwanted partner, for sexual lust, for desire to inflict cruelty on someone smaller, a child. Sometimes son kills father, father son. On rare occasions even mother has killed child but that is usually because she suffers from post-natal depression or mental illness. Rarest of all is the son who kills his mother.

It is usually for money and that means that the son must come from a family that has money to make it worthwhile. The ordinary son, from whatever family, would no more think of harming his mother than anything else in the world. Even amongst the hardened professional criminal classes mother is sacrosanct. Mothers are often called as witnesses to testify that their son was a marvellous boy, always good to his mum, always kind and considerate and never any trouble. Although the phrases are a cliché, hackneyed and chipped away into public phraseology like 'you know what I mean', 'over the moon', 'you must be joking' and 'sick as a parrot' they are genuine. Mothers are revered and honoured all over the world.

Those, therefore, who do kill their dear old mums are regarded as the worst kind of killers, even worse than those who kill children in a revolting way like the four men who, in 1989, were jailed for long periods for the manslaughter of one of their rent boys, a lad of fourteen.

One such killer was a boy called Andrew Alder, aged twenty, who shot dead both his parents for their money, for his inheritance which had to be shared with his sister. He committed his terrible crime early in the eighties in a tiny village outside Chichester, Sussex, coming home from his studies at a Hertfordshire polytechnic to stage a robbery of the family silver to cover his appalling deed. His father was a retired senior naval officer who had served in intelligence in the East with distinction. They were well known to a large circle of friends. Andrew came home and killed them. He walked into his father's room and blew him to pieces. His mother lay in the next room knowing what her only son was obviously going to do to her.

She was right. As he walked in with his shotgun she put her arm over her face to protect herself and said 'Oh Andrew' but it made no difference. He plastered the wall with her head and then went back to college, having hidden the gun on the old RAF wartime Battle of Britain airfield at Tangmere near his home.

Police at first suspected a burglar being disturbed but it did not add up and when he was questioned the son – who had been drinking with friends the lunchtime after he had killed – confessed and pleaded guilty to murder at his trial when he was jailed for life. He showed little remorse at the trial and went to the cells without shame. The irony was that by killing his parents for their money he disqualified himself from his inheritance. His sister got the lot.

He is nothing to do with the Triangle; I mention him only to show that in the rare but vicious business of mother-killing he is an example, though by no means the worst in the history of the crime.

Jeremy Bamber who lived in the Triangle, a handsome dark-haired young man whose presence sent girls weak at the knees, whose dark eyes could reduce them to jelly, was far worse. He hated all his close relatives and finished them off.

He was born illegitimate in 1961 and was sent for adoption by his mother, a south coast vicar's daughter. Six weeks after his birth he was adopted by Nevill and June

Bamber, a well-off farming family in Tolleshunt D'Arcy. Nevill and June Bamber were then thirty-six, very much part of the local community, he a wartime fighter pilot much liked and soon to become a magistrate, she a pillar of the Church, becoming more and more so as time went on. Their other adopted child, Sheila, also the illegitimate child of a clerical family, caused them problems with her behaviour. She was three years older than Jeremy.

He grew up a normal boy at first, going to primary school at Maldon where he fought and played and enjoyed himself with the other boys. When he was eleven he was sent to Gresham's School, Holt, a well-known Norfolk public school where he learnt, among other things, to shoot.

By sending him to boarding-school the Bambers made a fatal mistake. He just could not understand why they should go to the trouble to adopt him and then send him away from home. It was an understandable viewpoint. Many a small boy has cried himself to sleep at his prep school, terrified by being sent into the great wide world when aged only seven or eight, removed by his parents from the protection and love of their home into a hostile, cold environment from which he learns very quickly he will never return for the rest of his childhood except for holidays. It is a shock that most get over but for some it remains with them for the rest of their lives, the feeling of not being really wanted, that home and parenthood is a sham and the quicker the child is out of the house and out of sight the better. A learned headmaster once said that some boys who go through the public-school system put up a defence to hide their emotions and that it never comes down, making it impossible for them to really love. It may cause resentment against their parents, it may tilt the balance to crave for extra loving or it may – as it did in Jeremy Bamber's heart for he had more reason than most, having been adopted especially to give him a home – cause hatred and if strong enough, create stress and loathing that can result in disaster.

At Gresham's, Bamber was no one special but did well with his gun in the cadet force and had the reputation of being a loner and a bit of a bully. People often remember only the worse years later when they are called upon to recall a school mate who is in trouble. Others remember good and bad.

He left school without any qualifications and went to Colchester College where he got seven GCE O levels and his reputation as a ladies' man began to grow.

After that he set off for Australia to see the Far Country on his savings and had a marvellous time. He moved on to New Zealand where again he led the good life but at the same time doing a commercial driving course and learning more about farming.

Nevill was determined that his son whose Latin good looks were becoming more and more apparent as he passed through adolescence and puberty into manhood, should follow him as a farmer. He and his wife who could not have children of their own, lavished all their love on the two children they had adopted and wanted only the best for them.

Jeremy looked as though he would make the grade but Sheila was another matter. She was volatile, temperamental, wilful and suffering from a mental illness that caused her to be expelled from two schools. As time went on she became worse and when she was caught in a compromising position with a man by her mother when the girl was seventeen, she was called 'the devil's child'.

Sheila went to London where her father bought her a flat and she trained to be a hairdresser and then had a brief career as a model. The fact that his father had bought his sister a flat caused even more resentment to Bamber who had been given a 48-acre farm and a cottage in Goldhanger near the family home. It was his father's reward for his hard work on White House Farm after his time in the Antipodes. It did not match up to the lifestyle he yearned, the fast cars like Porsches still just a dream on his £7,500 a year wage; he owned a Vauxhall Astra.

When the Bambers thought their boy would settle down he started to row with his father, sometimes furiously, over the big farm and when he could take it over. His father said that it was not time, that he would have to wait.

The son watched angrily as his father, almost the squire, walked the fields with his gun and his labrador, searching for rabbits, and his mother did her good church works, organizing visits to the sick and looking after the elderly. She was a churchwarden in the fourteenth-century church.

In his mind was the tiny seed of hatred that was beginning to grow. His parents were not really aware of it. They had problems with Sheila.

She married a potter in London and had twin boys, Nicholas and Daniel, in 1979. But the break-up of her marriage soon after depressed her and revived her mental illness. She was often in debt and even had girlie pictures taken to raise cash although she did not try to have them published.

But, according to her brother, she contemplated suicide several times and wanted to be with God. She said she was Joan of Arc, the Virgin Mary, wanted to lead CND and to go to heaven, taking people there with her when she went.

She certainly did find religion after going into a mental hospital for treatment for her depression and drug-taking. She had tried to kill herself and in March 1985 she was suffering from bizarre and paranoid ideas including believing she was a white witch whose task was to rid the world of evil.

In her religious beliefs she was helped by her mother who was spending more and more time within religion, going to revivalist meetings with her daughter and trying to help her back into a normal life where she could continue to be a loving mother – which she always was – of her twin boys.

Her mental state was a great help to Jeremy Bamber, vain and arrogant and not above adding to his attraction by the use of eyeliner, whose determination to get his hands on the farm and everything that went with it was growing. He confided as much to a schoolteacher called Julie, with whom he was living.

He told her that he was planning to kill the family. He had decided that his sister and mother were mad, his father decrepit and was not interested in the twins who lived with their mother and grandparents in the farmhouse. She did not believe him, thinking it was wild talk.

It was not.

Julie, aged twenty-two, was besotted with the Romeo who wooed all the girls. She listened to his grumblings, his growing complaints about his parents and what they had done to him and how unfair it was, about the mental illness of his sister who was known as Bambi in the modelling world, a beautiful dark-haired girl when in good health.

Bamber and Julie were together for twenty months and during that period her lover, who was highly sexed and could make love time after time, constantly talked about ways he could inherit the family money, which was about £400,000.

He had two ideas which he called Plan One and Plan Two. Plan One was a fiendish and fairly complicated operation involving feeding all five – father, mother, sister and the twins – his mother's sleeping pills and when they had taken them and were asleep he would set fire to the house by throwing a bottle of gin on the floor and setting fire to it. In that way the house would burn down and they would all die and he would inherit. He discovered a flaw to that. The house insurance was too low.

So he talked of his other plan which was far more simple and evil. He would go into the house and shoot every one of them and let people think that his mad sister Bambi who would be there at the time, was responsible.

Julie said later: 'He talked about his plans, all aimed at inheriting the family fortune, for months but I had never taken them seriously. You never believe in your wildest dreams that someone is actually going to murder their own family.

'He always had to be the centre of attention and I dismissed it as something outrageous that he thought would guarantee my attention. I'd just say "Oh yes Jeremy have a good night's sleep and you'll feel better in the morning."

'I never stopped to consider for one minute that he would ever seriously think of trying to get rid of his family.'

She was wrong, quite terrifyingly wrong. She was loving a calculating, evil man who was about to do just that and what is more he told her in advance on the evening of the dreadful crime. At ten in the evening of 6 August 1985 he rang her to say that he had decided it was now or never. She told him he was being foolish.

Five hours later she received another call from him. He made it after he rang the police. He told her 'Everything is going well. Something's wrong at the farm. Bye honey I love you lots.'

Something indeed was wrong at the farm, horrendously wrong, unbelievably wrong. No satanic film could convince audiences that what went on in that farmhouse in that quiet little Essex village that night was real.

The first the police knew that anything was wrong came in the early hours when Bamber rang them to say that his father had rung him in the early hours to say:

'Come quickly, Sheila has gone crazy, she has got a gun.'

His son rang Chelmsford police station, not dialling 999 but making an ordinary call. Then he rang Julie because he did not think the police were very interested in what he was telling them and because he needed a friendly ear before going to the house.

Outside it he found police waiting having overtaken the normally fast-driving young farmer; they waited for three hours in case the intruder was in there. During that time the worried but ever-willing son drew up plans of the house for the police, ready for the moment when they would storm in. He also took the opportunity to tell the armed officers about his sister's mental illness.

He was to say later: 'Within myself I was frightened. I wanted to know what had gone on. I don't think they understood the extent of Sheila's illness and I was trying to convince them that she was unpredictable. They asked me if she had used guns and I was trying to tell them there were lots of guns in the house and that she could have used any of them.'

One thing he did not tell them was that also in the house were the wills of his parents, his father leaving everything to him, his mother leaving everything to Bambi.

When the police finally went in they found a massacre. They broke in because the door was locked from the inside. The kitchen was in a terrible mess, clearly the scene of a struggle for survival. There was blood, a broken lampshade, pieces of rifle butt everywhere and a watch under the rug. And the body of Nevill Bamber.

He had been initially shot and wounded as he fought for his life. He was a big man, six foot four inches tall. His son was around six foot, his daughter five feet seven inches tall, his wife around the same. He had been beaten around the head and shot in the lip, through the jaw and the larynx, serious but not fatal wounds. These were caused by four shots. But he had been finished off with four more bullets carefully and accurately fired through his head.

The police went upstairs to the bedroom where the little twin boys had been sleeping. Daniel had five wounds to his head, his brother Nicholas three, both shot as they slept. It was awful but their search of the house was by no means finished, their discovery of death by no means over.

They went into the Bambers' bedroom where they found Mrs Bamber. It seemed that she had first been shot as she lay in bed but she had managed to get out of bed and blood had run down her legs onto the carpet as she walked in her death throes. She had seven wounds; in the knee, arm, chest, neck, forehead and between the eyes.

There was one more victim, Sheila, Bambi, the mentally ill one, the unpredictable girl who could do anything and wanted to rid the world of evil and take those she thought were evil to heaven with her.

She was lying in the same room as her mother. On top of her was a gun with a broken butt, an empty magazine and nothing in the breech. The semi-automatic rifle belonged to her father. He had bought it a year earlier with a telescopic sight and silencer.

There were two gunshot wounds to her neck, one of which had gone into her backbone.

Hardened policemen felt ill. It was carnage of the highest order, not normally associated with the country-side, certainly not in such numbers.

The evidence was hard and strong. Twenty-five shots had been fired in all, fifteen from close range, all accurate direct and unswerving on their target, the work of someone who knew all about guns and who had done their wicked work with skill and finesse.

It was also the work of someone who was not sane, not in normal mental health, more, a raving lunatic who could do this awful thing not just to two defenceless elderly adults, but to tiny sleeping twins, innocent tots who had been despatched with the brutality of a Nazi concentration-camp guard.

But among the dead was one who was quite capable of doing such an appalling act if the poison that her foster brother had been dripping into the ears of the police as they waited through dawn on that August morning, was true. She could shoot. There were guns in the house. She had a history of mental illness, treatment just a few weeks before in a mental hospital, threats of suicide, and, her brother had slipped in the information, violence to the twins.

The door was locked from the inside suggesting that it was an inside job and the person who could have committed it, who was number one in the frame, was inside with no sign of break-in and with the gun on her chest. Her fingerprints were on it and so were those of her father but he was lying dead downstairs after a tremendous battle to the death with his daughter, police considered, so that the lack of anyone else's fingerprints on the gun suggested that she was last to die.

That she was the murderer who had finished off her parents in a flash of lunacy, homicidal madness, and then her own children and finally herself, they were sure.

There was no need to look further. The detective chief inspector, a dedicated officer of the highest calibre, arrived from Chelmsford and as the man in charge of the case, studied all the evidence he had before him, listened to what his men had to tell him, what Jeremy Bamber had told them, considered it all and decided that it was an open and shut case. Bambi had killed them and then herself. There was no need to look further. The case was closed. He went off to play golf in a police charity match.

Within a few days the five, including Bambi, the berserk murderess, had been buried and cremated and that was, as far as the police were concerned, the end of the matter.

There would be an inquest and the verdict would be one of unlawful killing of Mr and Mrs Bamber and the twins and suicide by their mother.

The police were wrong. They had forgotten the relatives who were not going to allow the case to be closed without some attempt to look at the evidence, for as you will read the blunders were quite astonishing and could only have been made and matters overlooked by someone who was supremely confident there was nothing to solve or investigate further.

The family began to look themselves after distraught Jeremy had wept with his girlfriend (who knew a little of what had really happened) on his arm at the funeral of his parents and sister.

As Bamber began to enjoy himself, night clubbing, out with his girl and other girls, his relatives began to look more closely at what happened. They were regarded as the Miss Marple squad by police who thought they were wasting their time. So what did they find?

The first strange thing was that Jems, as his mother called him, did not ring 999 but made an ordinary call to the police station. Then there was the odd business of police racing at half-past three in the morning actually overtaking Bamber in his car on the way to the farm and they had to come twice as far as he had.

Because they believed that Bambi, a drug taker, was the killer they never checked to see whether there had been a break-in. It was only later when the truth began to come out that they noticed suspicious marks on window catches in the kitchen and the hacksaw blade the killer used to let himself in.

Then there was the state of Bambi's feet. Like the dog who did not bark in the Sherlock Holmes story it was a classic clue that was overlooked. For although she was supposed to have rampaged through the house of death, slaughtering as she went, there was no blood or dirt on her bare feet; not a speck of blood there at all.

Her father had been savagely beaten as he fought for his life. His skull was fractured and his eyes blackened. He was six feet four inches tall and his daughter was nine inches shorter. He was big and strong, a country farmer, she was small and on drugs and slight. How could she have done it?

She was supposed to have fired a total of twenty-five shots with precision as she went on the kill. But there was not a trace of gun oil on her hands or nightdress and her beautifully manicured fingernails were just as they should have been. A gun expert broke one of his finger nails as he tried to reload with the stiff mechanism. And she was a terrible shot. The killer was an expert. She was clumsy in most things she did.

Bamber told the police that he had used the gun that day to shoot rabbits and he left it lying around the house with the silencer and telescopic sight on it. There was no silencer on it when police found it lying on Bambi's body, on her chest with the barrel pointing carefully at her throat. The point about that was that she was not big enough to reach the trigger to fire the two shots that killed her.

And that was amazing because tests later, when police thought that perhaps she was not the killer after all, showed that one of the shots – and both could have proved fatal – was fired with the silencer on and the other with it off. If the police theory was right she had shot herself once with the silencer on, got up and hidden it, then gone back to the room and shot herself, this time fatally, with the silencer off.

Police searched for the silencer for three days without finding it. Bamber's cousin, David Boutflour, was in the house for three minutes before he found it in the gun cupboard. Forensic tests showed Bambi's hair on it. But how? Police took two days to come and collect the silencer and on the way to the laboratory managed to lose a vital clue: a grey hair on the silencer which undoubtedly belonged to Bambi.

It followed the pattern that the police had set. The squad of 40 officers who searched the house did not find a cartridge case under the wardrobe for two days and three officers actually looked in the gun cupboard where the silencer was but did not spot it.

They stripped all the bloodstained carpets and bedding from the house and burned them all, destroying vital forensic evidence should it have turned out that they were wrong about the killer. They even washed down the walls so that Bamber would not be upset when he returned.

They even handled the gun without wearing gloves and did not ask Bamber for his fingerprints for six weeks.

And on top of all that no one bothered to wonder how Bamber was able to phone the police while still connected to the farm where police found the receiver off the hook.

The police were unbelievably complacent and sadly the officer who believed Sheila alone was to blame died after falling from a ladder. But eventually even they were impressed by what the family had discovered. The problem was that they had accepted what Bamber had intended them to accept. He had planned carefully and prepared a scene and story that could be fed to the unsuspecting police. He told them about his nutty sister, his father ringing, the gun, that she had gone crazy and that police could see that there had been no sign of a break-in.

But what the family told them, what the family pointed out, what they too discovered was that, whatever else she may have been and done, Bambi loved her sons very much indeed and the only person who ever alleged or said that she had attacked them was Bamber. Everyone else said it was the last thing she would have done.

And what of Bamber? He was living the high life, still with his girlfriend who was becoming more and more upset about what she knew he said had happened and his part in it.

He sold some of the family possessions to pay off death duties, he said, but he lived well with fast cars and drinks. He was Jack the Lad and even tried to sell his life story with the girlie pictures that Bambi had taken to the *Sun* for a four-figure sum. They turned him down.

His girlfriend was tortured with guilt. He had told her that someone else had done it for him. She was to say later:

'He told me the police had told him it was an open and shut case. If the police were convinced why should they believe me?

'I was scared of what Bamber would do to me. But I

could not cope with his guilt and that is why I went to the police.'

It was the start of the end for Jems who had thought he was safe from the police who had been so good to him, who had even drunk with him after the murders.

He of course denied it and has denied it vehemently ever since.

But added to the evidence that the relatives had provided was the dramatic and damning statement that his girlfriend gave to the police. For she could no longer live with the terrible secret that she shared with her lover.

It was not that he admitted to her that he had killed his families. The secret was that he had paid a man £2,000 to do it for him, explaining: 'I couldn't have done it.'

The man he falsely accused of carrying out the contract killing for him was Matthew MacDonald, who, according to Julie, was supposed to be a mercenary. She claimed that Bamber told her he had paid the man £2,000 but when Mr MacDonald gave evidence at Chelmsford crown court it turned out that he was a plumber who had certainly worked abroad as a contract manager but had never been in any army.

At the trial the jury heard how Julie went to the police only after she and Bamber had quarrelled. The prosecutor said:

'The guilt of the knowledge began to weigh on her. At one stage in a restaurant he told her he had no feelings of guilt about the killings and she said if he felt like that there must be something wrong with him.'

In her statement Julie, who knew Bamber's mother referred to her as 'a harlot' said:

'From the beginning he was trying to commit the perfect murder. His original plan was to give them drugs with drinks and shoot them and set fire to the house.

'He would make it look as though his father had fallen asleep with a cigarette. He decided against this because he discovered the insurance on the house was too low.'

The girl who after the trial said that she was incapable of making love to Bamber after the deaths, went on to say that he decided later to stage the killings and make it look as if Sheila had gone mad.

The prosecutor told the jury at the trial in October 1986, long after the murders:

'On 6 August at 10 p.m. Bamber called her and said it was now or never.

'She told him he was being foolish. At 3 a.m. she received another call from Bamber before he called the police.

'He told her, "Everything is going well, don't worry. Something's wrong at the farm. Bye honey, I love you lots."

'Shortly after the killings Bamber embraced her at his house and laughed. It was indeed a chuckle.

'He had just said to her, "I should have been an actor."

'Later that day she asked Bamber if he had done it. He replied, "No I couldn't have done it" and said he had paid Malcolm MacDonald to do it. But, said the prosecutor, at the time Mr MacDonald was at home with his girlfriend.

Julie, he said, did not go to the police until a month after the shootings after a row. When the trial was over she said that Bamber made no attempt to stop her going to the police and told her, 'Honey you know my life is in your hands' and when they talked for the last time he said, 'I hope you realize that you'll never meet anyone who loves you as much as I do.'

In court she denied trying to make the evidence as black as she could for her former lover. She made strange claims, such as that Bamber strangled rats with his hands because he wanted to test his resolve.

She said: 'He resented his mother for sending him away to boarding-school and said he never ever forgave her for that. He could not see how she could adopt a child and then send it away to boarding-school.

'She said that she never showed him any affection. He regarded her as a maniac and he blamed her for making Sheila mad.'

The jury heard how Bamber behaved after the murders, how he told the police about Bambi's mental state, how he gave police permission on the day of the killings to destroy bloodstained items in the eighteenth-century house, how two days later he asked for a sequence of deaths because according to legal advice he had received this would have a bearing on his parents' wills. He also discussed the Porsche he wanted in place of his Vauxhall and how he was going to live the good life.

She said that she helped Bamber choose furniture and decorate the cottage his parents had bought in Goldhanger, a hamlet near the farm. She said:

'I saw his parents occasionally but not often because they disapproved and his mother thought I was a loose woman.'

Her lover resented his parents because they tried to control his life and tell him what to do and thought he was not working hard enough on the farm. She said that between July and October 1984 Bamber said his parents 'were getting down his throat' and he often wished he could get rid of them.

'Initially it was just his parents but later it was also Sheila and the twins.

'Basically the reason behind it was that his father was getting old and his mother was mad anyway and he would put her out of her misery.

'Sheila was mad as well and had nothing to live for and the twins were emotionally disturbed and unbalanced.

'Then between October and December 1984 he became more specific and talked of several methods of getting rid of them.

'He said he would drug their drinks using his mother's tranquillizers and then they would go to sleep. He would return to the house by bicycle and burn the house down using alcohol.

'I said it was ridiculous to try and burn the house down. It was too beautiful and too big to set alight easily. Then he told me he had changed his mind and said that some valuable things in the house weren't insured. He mentioned a Meissen clock under Mr and Mrs Bamber's bed.

'Later he said he would do it by shooting. He told me how he would get in and out of the house. He said Sheila would be the scapegoat because she had been in a mental hospital.'

She said that after the shootings, after he had come home and cuddled her, she did not tell anyone about the conversations about the murders because she did not take them seriously.

She explained to the jury in the packed courtroom where everyone listened intently to the astonishing story that unfolded over the days:

'I loved him. Initially I didn't want to believe that he had got rid of his family in that way. I was scared myself to believe it. Jeremy said that if anything happened it would also happen to me because I knew about it. He said that if I ever said anything I could be implicated in the crime as well as him.'

And for the funerals – for which he bought himself an expensive designer suit and a £30 tie – he put on white make-up to look more drawn. He joked on the eve of them as he set the video so he could watch himself. He said he hoped that the cameras would get his good side.

Bamber listened to all this and before giving his side of the accusations against him heard his counsel Mr Geoffrey Rivlin, QC say to Julie:

'I put it to you that all this about him planning murders and doing these terrible things came into your mind when it became clear that Jeremy didn't want to marry you?'

Not so, the student teacher declared. 'I am afraid you are totally incorrect,' she said.

Not so, said Bamber when he went, smartly suited, incredibly attractive, into the witness box. He said that their relationship was over and she had gone to the police making up allegations 'out of spite because of the splitting up' and he had sent her a love note believing she would take back the accusations.

His counsel had told the jury in his opening speech for the defence that Sheila was very sick, believing that she was being taken over by the devil and that her twin baby sons would try to seduce and murder her unless they were killed first. She felt she was locked in a coven of evil and that she was a white witch with a mission to conquer it.

At various times she thought she was the Virgin Mary or Joan of Arc or the leader of the CND. She was also capable of extreme violence, ranting and raving, beating the walls with her fists and threatening to kill herself.

Her 'incredible' mental state at the time of the killings in August 1985 was the key to the murders, Mr Rivlin suggested to the jury. She had twice been treated in hospital for psychotic symptoms and suffered from a mental disorder which caused her to lose contact with reality and suffer delusions and hallucinations and had the morbid idea that the twins were reacting to an evil force within her.

This view was later in the trial to be supported by a psychiatrist who said that once branded the Devil's Child by her mother who caught her in a sex incident, Bambi became obsessed with the demonic power of evil. He said:

'The essential theme of her illness was that evil emanated from her mind and from her adoptive mother. These were morbid and abnormal thoughts.'

A boyfriend told the jury via a written statement that she thought her telephone was bugged and that the devil was sitting opposite her and he added: 'She had a deep and intense dislike of her mother. She said her mother was always quoting religion at her and telling her it was wrong to make love to her boyfriends.'

Then Jeremy Bamber gave evidence. He looked smart, assured and handsome but he spoke so quietly as he answered question after question that he often had to be asked to speak up so that the jury could hear, even in the still of the courtroom where everyone was silent so that they could hear what this young man charged with five unthinkable murders had to say.

No, he declared, he had not murdered any of his family, indeed his relationship with them was a loving one even though there had been a lack of understanding between him and his mother because it had not been easy to cope with her religion.

He whispered that there was no animosity between him and his sister, Sheila, 'Bambi', but he found it difficult to cope with her bizarre behaviour describing how she alternated between believing she was Joan of Arc, the Virgin Mary and the leader of the Campaign for Nuclear Disarmament. She contemplated suicide and was violent to the twins, the only time anyone ever mentioned such a thing. He said:

'She wanted to be with God. She wanted to go to heaven. She wanted to take people with her and she wanted to save the world.'

When he was asked if he was using her mental illness as a cover for what he had done he denied it.

He also spoke of his girlfriend and why she should tell stories about him – which he said were untrue. He said:

'She has been telling a great number of lies. The reason was jilted love and she did it out of spite. I believe she was telling the police stories about me out of spite because we were splitting up.'

It came about because they had a violent row over a phone call from an ex-girlfriend. He said that Julie became 'really jealous' and grabbed the phone and then stormed into the bedroom where she broke a mirror.

When the other girl rang back she attacked him in fury. 'I had never seen her in a rage like that. She smashed me round the face twice' and when he tried to restrain her she said she would go to the police if he hit her.

But he said that he did send her a love note after his arrest in which he said he was sorry that they had parted. He did it, he explained, believing that she would take everything back.

On the night of the murder, he said, he was at home watching television and he denied ever saying that 'tonight is the night' for killing his parents.

In the early hours he was woken by a call from his father who said, 'Come quickly, Sheila's gone crazy, she's got a gun.'

He had no chance to speak himself and when he tried to phone his father back the line went dead and he got the engaged tone so he phoned the police to report the call before phoning Julie. It never entered his head, he said, to dial 999.

And he phoned Julie because 'I was very worried. The police didn't seem interested. I telephoned her because I needed a friendly ear. I told her there was trouble at the farm and I remember she was talking as if she thought the whole thing was a practical joke.'

He declared he never said things were going well nor had he ever told his uncle he could easily kill his parents as the prosecution had also alleged.

It was while he waited with police for three hours outside his parents' home because the police thought the intruder might still be inside with a gun, that he told them about his sister's mental condition. He said:

'Within myself I was frightened. I wanted to know what had gone on. I don't think they understood the extent of Sheila's illness and I was trying to convince them she was very unpredictable.

'They asked me if she had used guns. I was trying to tell them there were lots of guns in the house and that she could have used any of them.'

When the police eventually went into the farmhouse he stayed outside 'because that's where Mum and Dad died.'

He said he remembered someone giving him a whisky and him retching when he was told about the mass murders. He also had a drink with some police officers who called at his house the next day.

'I was in a state of shock, sometimes I believed what had gone on and sometimes I didn't,' he said, fighting back tears.

He denied the allegations against him such as telling police to remove and destroy the bloodstained furnishings because it was at their suggestion, that he had told Julie he should have been an actor and that he chuckled.

And he insisted that Bambi – who, the jury had heard, was locked in 'curtains of evil' – had punched one of the twins full in the face with her fist, but her violence was kept a family secret. And who could say, the jury might have wondered, because there was no one left apart from Jems to tell.

He also said that he had sold valuable items from the house including silver, china, guns and paintings but that was to raise money to pay the death duties so that he did not have to sell the house or farm.

He admitted he had read his parents' wills four or five years earlier. He also knew how his mother felt about him for earlier in the trial the sole executor of his parents' estate had read out a letter from his mother which reduced him to tears. It said:

'My darlings Nevill, Sheila and Jem,

'Should anything happen to me and I have left you, I write to tell you of my love for you all and for all you have given to me. All I pray is that God will love and protect you through the years ahead and hope, God willing, we may meet again my loves. Always my darlings, Mums.'

Bamber left the witness box, final speeches were made by counsel for both the prosecution and defence and then the judge, Mr Justice Drake, summed up, pointing to certain facts the jury – who had to decide whether it was mentally unstable Bambi or her smooth, handsome brother who had done this crime – might want to take into account.

Like the murder of their father. The judge said that whoever killed him had fought him first, using the butt of the rifle to inflict serious injuries on him.

But, said the judge, Sheila who was at first suspected was small and slight while her father was a six foot four inches tall heavily built farmer. He went on:

'These things are not conclusive but point to it being very unlikely indeed that she fought and overcame that tough farmer who managed to go on fighting apparently even with a number of wounds.'

Bamber, he said, had ample time – if indeed he was the killer – to go home and clean himself up before presenting himself to the police. And according to the defence version of what had happened her father would have had to fight while wounded and then be killed which left Sheila twenty-two minutes altogether to kill him, the rest of the family, remove the silencer and hide it, and go and wash before killing herself. The only blood on the silencer was hers, he told the jury. And she bore no marks from the fight and her fingernails and hands were undamaged from the shootings.

She was quite clearly a disturbed woman but the psychiatrist felt, the judge added, she could not have killed her six-year-old twins.

There was Julie, the judge pointed out, whom Bamber said was a woman scorned. She denied this but if hers was the only evidence against Bamber the jury would have to treat what she said with caution. But there was other evidence.

It took the jury over nine hours to convict Bamber. He looked pale but otherwise showed no emotion as he stood in the crumpled blue suit he had worn every day of the three-week trial. He showed no emotion either as the judge sentenced him to five life sentences with a recommendation that he served a minimum of twenty-five years.

Mr Justice Drake told him:

'Your conduct in planning and carrying out the killing of five members of your family was evil almost beyond belief. It shows that you, young though you are, have a warped, callous and evil mind concealed beneath an outwardly presentable and civilized manner.

'You killed your mother, you killed your father, you killed your sister – each alone would have been a dreadful crime. You fired shot after shot into them and also into two little boys, aged six, whom you murdered in cold blood while they were asleep in their beds.'

He went on: 'I believe you did so partly out of greed because, although you were well off for your age, you were impatient for more money and possessions.

'But I believe you also killed out of an arrogance in your character which made you resent any form of parental restriction or criticism of your behaviour.

'I believe you wanted at once to be the master of your own life as well as to enjoy the inheritance which would have come to you in the fullness of time.

'On imposing on you five life sentences which are fixed by law for murder I have to consider when I think it will be likely for it to be safe for you to be released from prison into the community.

'I find it difficult to foresee whether it will ever be safe to release into the community someone who can plan and kill five members of their family and shoot two little boys asleep in their beds.'

Bamber went to the cells knowing he had lost the inheritance he so craved.

That went to relatives who neither expected nor ever wanted it.

After the case there were recriminations about how the police bungled the investigation. They admitted that they were duped by Bamber in the early stages of the inquiry and the experts involved considered that the murder-suicide theory was possible.

A senior Essex officer said: 'With the benefit of that perfect science, hindsight, it could be said that the judgements made at the scene of the crime by senior officers were misdirected. But I must again emphasize the careful way in which the whole affair had been planned.'

As the judge put it, 'The perfunctory examination carried out by the police is only explicable because they thought there was nothing left to solve.'

Their assumption that it was Bambi who was responsible, their failure to look further than their noses, their bungling with clues and being bamboozled by the suave real killer led to a major inquiry in the force and a change in rules from the Home Office.

With that perfect science, hindsight, it is easy to blame the police for their ineptitude but at the same time the whole story was fed to them and the facts fitted the story and most people, even experts, would have been lulled into a sense of accepting at face value what they were told. Even, at a much higher level, the Germans accepted what they were fed by The Man who never was, by the spy Cicero and others. It is always easy to cast the first stone provided you do not have to sweep up the glass.

After the trial, as Bamber prepared his appeal, hunting for new evidence that would confirm what he said was true – evidence that so far has not made any difference to his conviction – newspapers produced lengthy backgrounds about the case.

Like Bambi, they too had probed her background to discover who she really was and where she came from. Bambi had found her real mother and had spent a week with her five months before she was murdered. Bambi was thrilled and so was her mother because they got on so well together and the years had bridged the scandal that led to Bambi's adoption via the Church of England Children's Society by the Bambers, who were vetted and came up to the high standards that her real mother's family required – a loving Christian family.

For Bambi's real mother was the daughter of a canon in the Church of England who had played an important role in the Queen's coronation in 1953. After the adoption Bambi's real grandparents went to Canada with the daughter who – in those days – was felt to have brought shame on the family. Later, because Bambi tracked her half brother, she managed to meet her mother. After her death her grandfather, now retired, held a prayer session in a cathedral in Canada and asked for the peace of the soul of his granddaughter.

And Jeremy Bamber? He too came from a Church of England family. His mother was the daughter of a vicar, his father a married army sergeant. Their brief affair ended with the birth of the mass killer who headed the terrible Triangle list of evil twenty-four years after he was adopted by the loving Bambers.

14

Murders in the Family

Some domestic murders occur in the heat of the moment. Others come as hatred or dislike or another love intervenes, necessitating the disposal of the partner. In the Triangle, over the years, there have been several domestic murders, some of no particular outside interest except for the tragedy of a life being taken, a family broken up, children left without their parents, one dead, the other in prison or even taking their life too.

The case of the Smiths (not their real name because the children are now grown up and it certainly was not their fault) was different.

It began on a Saturday night in 1963 when auburn-haired Sarah Smith's husband Geoffrey went out for the evening with his brother Reg, not for a drink or a meal but to find a house to rob.

They had house-breaking tools and a loaded revolver as a morale booster but, they were to insist later, nothing else. They never intended to use it. Sarah stayed in to look after the children at their Colchester home. She was an attractive young woman, friendly and chatty.

Her husband Geoffrey, a 31-year-old general labourer, and his brother, six years older, roamed around town looking for somewhere to rob.

That night the safe was blown in the Colchester Co-op and over £1,100 was stolen. The thief had a sense of humour for he left a note saying: 'Drink up. Best of luck from the Fiddlers Three. Take our advice – send for Lockhart.' He was one of the top television fictional detectives at the time. The police did not send for him however, but for Scotland Yard's forensic team who thought the note might have been written by Reg Smith, a fact he strongly denied.

However, he and his brother were picked up by police as they drove round town, near a store where there was a safe. They arrested the two men and put them in the back of the police car. They were handcuffed and separated on the back seat by Detective Inspector Harry Batson so that they were unable to do anything on the drive to the police station.

When they arrived they were searched.

In Reg's sock was a loaded Smith and Wesson .38 revolver and in his pocket was a full safe-blowing kit including enough gelignite to blow two safes – and five rounds of ammunition. They denied they were responsible for the Co-op safe-blowing.

The police went round to the Smiths' home and began searching. They found what they were looking for when they opened Sarah's handbag. In her gold-plated compact was powder – gunpowder, enough to blow two safes. In a muslin bag in her handbag was the arsenal for the revolver – 36 rounds of .38.

She told the detectives that she had never seen them there before and had no idea how the explosives got into her powder compact. She was charged with conspiring with her brother and brother-in-law to steal and to receiving the ammunition and one and a quarter ounces of gelignite. Her story that she had no idea how they got there was not accepted by the police.

However, her husband backed up her story. He said that she did not know that the arsenal was in her bag and that it was he who put it there.

Nevertheless, when the three appeared before the magistrates' court in the early summer she was sent for trial to the old Essex assizes which sat at Chelmsford.

In those days, before the change in the system whereby the old assizes and the quarter sessions which dealt with the less serious charges were made into one crown court, there was something more dramatic about the occasion. Perhaps it was because there were not so many cases to be tried so that there would only be one red robe judge, the high court judge, who came to town and went to a service. He then walked from Chelmsford Cathedral to the court where the Writ of Assize was read, a marvellous document which dated back to the Plantagenets, before he got down to work.

Now there are many courts for judges and justice is like a battery factory, defendants coming in and out of the dock with a regularity that can be overwhelming to someone who is not used to courts. So heavy is the amount of crime now that some courts sit throughout the summer holiday. There is a workmanlike approach that was not there before.

People arriving at the crown court no doubt still do so with terror and fear in their hearts, knowing that there will be retribution for what they have done. Families who come with them, hoping for the best, dreading and knowing that it will be the worst, remain almost anonymous unless it is a major case because there are so many others in the same plight. Twenty years ago it was not so.

The old Essex quarter sessions, which went back decades, covered part of east London including Romford which then was part of the Essex police force area. Families would come down as a day outing to see Dad – or even the son – come up before the court and go down before going over to the nearby hotel or pub for a drink to toast his courage in taking his medicine. Many East End criminal families would bring sandwiches in old-fashioned brown paper carrier bags for their day out. They accepted that this was the way of things in their lives and they stood out because there were so few people at the courts, so many less cases to be heard than today.

The chairman and his deputies at the sessions seemed to have more time, more personality. One, an engineer who had become a lawyer, liked to give people a chance but woe betide them if they did not take it. A pretty girl who had become entangled with a house-breaking gang was allowed to go free because he felt she would do better putting out her husband's slippers (oh! the innocence of those days thirty years ago) than sitting in a cell at Holloway. She went away and ignored what he had said. When she came back she went to jail.

The parade that went up and down the cell stairs was

slower. One man who had an affair with an under-age girl was allowed to go free when his wife came and said she would have him back. She scowled as she said it and the chairman said that he hoped she would greet her husband with a smile, which was more than she had given him.

Another woman pleaded guilty to shoplifting, a whole string of offences, but had not told her husband that she was up in court and facing almost certain imprisonment. The chairman insisted her husband be brought to court and the astonished man arrived to find his wife facing twelve months and no one to look after the children or him. She was put on probation.

Geoffrey and Reg Smith were in custody when they arrived at Chelmsford and were kept in the cells below the dock – where one defendant once did a victory jig after being found not guilty, clasping his hands high above his head like a boxer. Sarah was on bail and she arrived looking very smart.

Her brother-in-law was defended by the late Duncan Macrae, a man with some wit and a dry sense of humour. He was once in another case involving possessing house-breaking implements, but prosecuting. The police officer in the case described how he had found a jemmy and other tools including a pair of white gloves. The defending barrister who was a baronet, leapt to his feet and said it was a leading question when Mr Macrae asked if the police officer thought they were for use in house-breaking. Mr Macrae said he would rephrase the question and asked: 'Can you think of any other use for a white pair of gloves with those implements unless it is in case you meet a baronet and want to shake hands with him?'

All three Smiths denied the charges and the evidence was given about Sarah's handbag. But her barrister argued that, coupled with her husband's statement, there was no evidence that she knew it was there.

The late John Marriage, later a QC and chairman of the Bar before his early death, said on behalf of her husband: 'It was his fault his wife was charged and he has instructed me all along that what happens to him matters not; it was his wife he was worried about.'

The judge accepted the point and she was ordered to be discharged.

Her husband, who had a history of dishonesty and was on probation when he committed the offences for which he was now standing trial, and his brother then changed their pleas.

They admitted being in possession of house-breaking implements and the loaded revolver. The prosecution accepted the pleas and dropped the charges of conspiracy against both of them and the charge of raiding the Co-op office against Reginald.

Geoffrey was sentenced to a total of three and a half years, his elder brother to a total of two and a half years. The judge, Mr Justice McNair, told them:

'It must be made quite plain to everyone that the possession of a loaded revolver at night by men out on a house-breaking expedition will always be regarded by the court as a very grave matter indeed.

'You were well equipped to carry out house-breaking or safe-blowing and armed with a revolver which, whether you intended to use it or not, might have been used by you in the stress of apprehension or discovery.'

They went off to prison and Sarah went home to look after their two children, a girl and a boy, both of whom they adored.

While her man was locked up Sarah not unnaturally began to play. She was a popular, effervescent woman and she liked company. She began to get a small reputation which grew after Geoffrey came out of jail. Her unfaithfulness grew and so did his concern for what it might do to the children, who were not even teenagers, if their mother continued to bring her friends home to the house.

When he protested she threatened that she would kill herself and the children, knowing he adored them.

One morning, after the children had gone to school, he and his wife had it out in the kitchen, he shouting that she must stop bringing the men to the house and to think what effect it was having on the children, she ignoring him.

The end was almost inevitable. He lost his rag and

armed with a green plaited cord strangled her. The girl who had the arsenal in her powder compact lay on the floor in the lounge of their council house and the children had no mother any more.

Nor indeed a father, for he was taken down to the police station he knew well to be charged with the murder of his wife. Eventually he was back in the dock at Essex assizes to deny the charge and say that he had done it accidentally when he lost his self-control trying to frighten her into stopping bringing men back to the house, because he feared the succession of men who arrived with her might corrupt the children.

Mr William Howard QC defending, told the jury about Smith's feelings towards his children. He urged them to find him guilty of manslaughter, not murder, because of the provocation of his wife's unfaithfulness and the hold she had over him by threatening to take her own life and the children's.

The judge then told the jury to put moral judgement and sympathy out of their minds but it took them only thirty-five minutes to find Smith not guilty of murder but guilty of the lesser offence of manslaughter.

Then his eight previous convictions were read out before the judge told him:

'The jury has found you guilty of manslaughter. In doing so they took into account the very difficult circumstances of your married life and it was for that reason you were not convicted of the more serious crime.

'You were responsible for taking your wife's life and the taking of a human life is always a serious matter', and this manslaughter fell into the graver category of taking human life under provocation on the spur of the moment.

Alfred Jones (not his real name) was another who wanted to punish his wife, not in her case because she was unfaithful. He believed she failed to give him the sympathy and understanding he felt he deserved in the crippled state in which he was left after an accident with a pair of shears which lacerated his armpit, causing seven years of hospital treatment and agonizing pain.

Her punishment was a blast in the legs with a shotgun

as she ran for safety with her children at Eight Ash Green the day after Guy Fawkes Night in the late fifties.

It had not been a happy marriage. His character, it was said at Essex assizes where he pleaded guilty to wounding his wife with intent to cause grievous bodily harm, changed after he banged his head at the age of eighteen when jumping from a moving train.

He was born in Suffolk but grew up in Yorkshire where he married his first wife in the 1920s. She divorced him during the Second World War while he was a Colchester factory worker and she later died.

He married his second wife Phyllis in the last year of the war and they had a son four years later. In 1946 he was working as a handyman on a Suffolk farm when he had his accident with shears and was paid £1,700 compensation. He did not work properly for the next seven years because he was receiving treatment periodically in local hospitals.

His wife left him in 1956. He was so angry that he waylaid her as she fed her chickens and beat her with a stick. It was approaching the culmination of a marriage that had been unhappy from the start.

On 6 November he was given a lift to Eight Ash Green, the same village where Mary Kriek was abducted, and he was carrying a parcel in which he had a gun.

He slammed the barrel through a panel in the front door and fired, hitting his 77-year-old mother-in-law in the ankle.

Then his wife and his father-in-law, aged eighty-eight – 'a gallant old gentleman' the judge heard in the Chelmsford court – struggled with the double barrel of the twelve-bore as Jones fired through the window of the pantry and then again as he tried to get through the front door.

Then he roared at his wife: 'Now you are going to get it.'

She pushed three children who were with her – including her son – into the kitchen and then the gun fired again and she fell to the floor with her leg bleeding profusely from gunshot wounds.

Jones vanished and was not seen again for nearly three months.

During that time two things happened. Eighteen days after the shooting his mother-in-law died from an embolism and initially, when he was captured still making threats against his wife, he was charged with her murder.

But at his trial Mr Cyril Salmon QC, prosecuting, said: 'I have come to the conclusion that it would not be right for the Crown to offer any evidence on this charge.'

He explained that the old lady had died as a result of an embolism after pellets from the shotgun fired through the broken glass entered her ankle. But, he went on: 'She suffered thrombosis in each leg. The pellets had entered her left foot.

'Dr Camps [Home Office pathologist Dr Francis Camps] tells me it is impossible to say whether the embolism that killed her – a clot of blood detached from the thrombosis – came from the right leg or the left and he also says that it is impossible to say that the thrombosis in the right leg was caused by the gunshot in the left leg. Although death followed the wound it was some eighteen or nineteen days later.

'It would not appear that there is any evidence on which to ask a jury to say that death was caused by the wound.'

The second thing that happened while Jones, a man with a long list of convictions for theft, fraud and dishonesty, was on the run in the countryside and counties he knew so well, was that doctors fought to save his wife's leg.

By the time he was tried the wound had almost healed but the damage to the nerves which had been destroyed was such that at some time in the future it might have to be amputated so that she could walk relatively normally. The wicked way in which he had attacked her caused terror and pain far beyond the normal.

His feelings stayed the same after the shooting. He wrote her a threatening letter while on the run and even when arrested by the police. Another letter he wrote to his wife was his undoing. He gave it to a bus conductor to deliver to the terrified woman and the conductor told the police.

So how did this husband with a massive chip on his shoulder feel about it now, in front of a judge to whom he had admitted wounding with intent to do grievous bodily harm, his plea of not guilty to wounding with intent to commit murder having been accepted by the court? In that way a trial did not need to be held, Mrs Jones did not need to give evidence and public time and money was not wasted.

In any event the maximum sentences were the same: life.

Mr John Llewellyn, defending Jones, a balding, surly man, said:

'He is very conscious of the extremely grave position in which he stands. Nothing I say should be taken as a mitigation of the crime of which he now stands accused.

'My only purpose is to lay bare a few observations on the background to the case.

'You have heard of the two accidents. He had seven years' hospital treatment as a result of the accident with the shears and suffered agony.

'The second marriage turned out to be unhappy. The defendant thought that his wife failed to give him the sympathy and understanding which he felt he deserved in his crippled state.

'He has since claimed that he is attached to the boy. He felt very unhappy after his wife had left him with only the remnants of his compensation to live on and having to sleep rough at times.

'The time came, when embittered against his wife and in-laws, he contemplated suicide. It was with that in mind that he bought a gun.

'He intended to shoot himself on the doorstep of his mother-in-law's home. But he found difficulty in manoeuvring the gun with one arm.

'He went to take one look at his son and then lost control of himself.'

The courtroom was very still as Mr Llewellyn went on. Jones sat in the dock looking sullen. Everyone was listening to every word.

'The shots were not fired with the intention of murdering his wife,' Mr Llewellyn said. 'He had the muddled thought that she had failed to appreciate his suffering and that he would make her appreciate it more.'

It takes a strange mind to equate an accident with a pair of shears and a wicked attempt with a shotgun at close range to punish your wife.

However, his counsel went on:

'He has had time to think and it is fair to say that his anger, dreadful and wicked though it was, is spent.

'He realizes that he now faces a long and terrible sentence.'

Mr Llewellyn's and Jones's realization and anticipation were well founded. The judge, Mr Justice Donovan, a former Labour MP, told Jones:

'The grievous wound, which may mean the losing of your wife's leg, makes this one of the worst cases of bodily harm that can be imagined.

'It is quite clear that you are a little unstable mentally. That is not your fault.

'The circumstances of the case make me pause before passing a sentence of life imprisonment. Indeed one pauses very long before it can be inflicted on anybody. I feel compelled however in this case to impose the maximum sentence.'

He added the comforting words that life did not necessarily mean that Jones would spend the rest of his days in prison but that when the home secretary of the day felt it was safe for him to be released he would do so.

Jones took in what had been said, looked straight at the judge and said:

'Right, sir. Thank you.'

Then, wearing the same raincoat and scarf in which he had been arrested, he went to the cells and his wife was helped from the court.

Smith killed his wife because he thought her unfaithfulness and the parade of men she brought home would corrupt the children. Jones wounded his wife so terribly that she would be crippled for life because she did not give him the sympathy he thought he deserved for his wound. Neither marriage was happy at the time when the deeds were done.

Another cause for domestic murder is the fear that, struck down by a terminal illness, the partner in the marriage might fall in love with someone else before or after the death.

Such was the case of Farmer Bell.

They say that two ley lines meet in Coggeshall, mysterious energy paths that connect places of supernatural powers. They say that such lines and such powers have an effect on the people who live in such places and that they behave in a different manner to others. We already know that Coggeshall folk have funny ways but they are not psychic or evil but merely daft. Witchcraft then. Several witches were burnt in the market square and some say that their ghosts roam the streets casting spells on all those that see them. A likely tale they say. Others dismiss such talk as stupid. There are those who say that one of the pubs is haunted, and others say more than one is haunted and so is the Paycocke House.

Perhaps, they conclude, the horrible goings-on like the murders, like a ring of indecency when the town's toilets were a meeting place for some respectable people who were homosexuals, are all down to the past and the evil has slipped down the centuries like a fog. Others would just say that it is human nature, as for instance, in the case of farmer Jimmy Bell, where a combination of human things made him do what he did.

He was a violent, jealous man. He was also rich and successful and had a magnificent house and one thousand acres in Coggeshall.

His first marriage was stormy. He claimed that his wife Janet was unfaithful. He claimed that she had told him that American servicemen had cut cards for her, the winner having sex with her. She absolutely denied this but Farmer Bell, forty-six years old, was adamant. She was guilty and he was not having it.

He hung toilet seats round her neck as a collar of shame and landed up in court where he was jailed for six months. He served only five weeks in 1982 before being released by a judge on appeal and waiting for him was the new love in his life, Augusta, aged seventeen, whom he met while she was working as a receptionist in a Norwich hotel. She was hypnotized by Bell, a millionaire and former clay-pigeon shooting champion.

The fact that he had dragged the first Mrs Bell round an American airbase with the toilet seat of shame round her neck did not worry Augusta. She said 'He's a wonderful man.'

Her older fiancé was quite clear how he felt. He said: 'She's the new love of my life. We are soon to be wed. She's a wonderful girl and the thought of her kept me going during those terrible weeks in prison ... As soon as my divorce is finalized we will marry.'

And marry they did. No one could ever say that the marriage was a smooth one. Perhaps it was the age gap because he was twenty-eight years older than his new bride. Perhaps it was because he was ill and knew that the cancer in his stomach was getting worse and worse. The birth of their daughter Victoria seemed to help but the rows did not stop. They merely got worse and worse and Augusta talked of going home to mother. The rows did not stop.

Perhaps it was because the radiotherapy to control the cancer did not do the trick that Bell became more aggressive, more violent, more argumentative. Whatever it was, Augusta finally went home to mother in Norfolk with baby Victoria.

Once there she refused to return. It signed her death warrant.

Her husband, knowing he had little time to live, went to see her and pleaded with her to come back to Coggeshall, back to Essex. She again refused.

Then she got an injunction preventing her husband from going to the house. But her husband who promised when they married that his hell-raising days were over, was not going to give up. Armed with his pump-action shotgun he drove to the house in Norfolk in June 1986, and forced his way in.

His wife and the baby and her mother, Sally, were in the kitchen when he arrived mad with rage and jealousy. He stormed in and began rowing. He and his wife fought as her mother and the baby watched.

Sally, the mother, told the inquest: 'They wrestled and she knocked him over backwards. He was sort of picking himself up and I took the initiative and just escaped with the baby.'

Her daughter, she said, 'Saved my life really'.

As she ran with the little girl, Sally, aged forty-eight, did not hear the shots that rang out across the countryside because the baby was screaming in terror.

There were two lots of shots. First Bell pumped them into his wife and when he was sure that she was dead he turned the gun on himself. The former champion shot made no mistake.

The coroner recorded a verdict that Augusta was unlawfully killed and that her husband shot himself while the balance of his mind was disturbed.

A friend said afterwards: 'It was bad enough fighting cancer without losing his wife. I think he snapped and decided if he was going so was she.'

Such killings coupled with suicides or attempted suicides are common. All over Britain and the rest of the world men shoot their women for any number of reasons. The only difference in the case of Jimmy Bell was that he came from Coggeshall and was just another statistic in that unhappy place.

And like all other murders in this book, they happened in such an ordinary, rural, quiet piece of the English countryside, small and lightly populated but – and who is to say why – tainted with the brush of murder, mayhem and violence.

A little plot of England that makes up the Essex Triangle.

Index